CODING

INTERVIEWS

GUIDE

Essential Guide to Prepare You with
the Most Effective Case Studies and
Coding Interview Questions

OLIVIA MILLER

Table of Contents

Introduction

What if you could learn everything you need to ace the coding interview in just a few hours?

You can.

This book will give you the tools and resources to prepare for your next coding interview and ace it easily. You'll learn how to prepare for your first coding interview and how to answer common questions.

This book is perfect for both newbies and experienced professionals alike.

Chapter 1

The Process of Interview

The job market is very competitive, and the first step in getting your dream job is to stand out from the crowd. One way to do this is by having a good interview. You'll have a better chance of landing an interview if you have some experience. If you haven't had any professional experience yet, consider volunteering with an organization that interests you or taking courses that will help develop relevant skill sets for your chosen field. Once you've earned some work experience and credentials behind your name, it's time to start preparing for that all-important in-person meeting with potential employers!

Find a Job That Matches Your Skill Set

- Research the company.

- Research the industry.

- Research the role.

- Research the interviewer(s).

- Research what you can about their interviewing style and background before you meet them in person (e.g., if they are a hiring manager or headhunter, etc.).

Prepare a Resume

- The first step is to prepare a professional-looking resume and CV. To begin, you should gather all of your relevant information (education history, work experience, etc.) and put it into a single document in reverse chronological order (i.e., most recent job first). You should also include any skills specifically related to the position you are applying for, such as foreign language fluency or computer proficiency.

- Hire an expert if necessary. If you don't feel comfortable formatting everything yourself or creating something very specific, like a cover letter or reference page on your own, consider hiring someone who knows how to do this sort of thing professionally.

Research the Company

Researching your interviewer is a great way to ensure that you're prepared for the interview and know what to expect. Here are some things to look into:

- **The company website** - This will give you an idea of what they do, how they do it, and who they are as a company. Many companies have a "Careers" section where they list job openings, which can be useful if an opening interests you.

- **Company culture** - Googling "[Company Name] Culture Reviews" will give insight into how employees feel about working at this particular company. You may also want to check Glassdoor or Indeed for reviews from former employees who have previously worked with this company.

- **Mission statement** - A mission statement defines what values are important to the organization and how it plans on achieving its goals moving forward. It could be something like "To provide every customer with 100% satisfaction on every purchase made!" Or maybe even more specific like "Provide quality products while maintaining profitability levels within our target market! We promise high-quality service because we care about each customer experience! If there is ever any issue or concern, please let us know so we can solve any problems immediately!

Prepare for the Interview Questions

Before you go into the interview:

1. Be prepared.

2. Make sure you know the company, who they are, and what they do.

3. Consider how your skills and experience can help them achieve their goals.

In addition to knowing the company, it is also important to know what they are looking for in an employee. Research their mission statement or social media posts to get a feel for who they are as an employer and what type of person would fit well with their organization.

Practice answering questions about yourself positively that highlight your strengths without bragging or being negative about other people or your past experiences. Be enthusiastic!

Practice Answering Typical Interview Questions

The best way to prepare for your interview is to practice answering common interview questions. Many websites and books can help you with this, or you could even ask a friend who has been through the process before.

When preparing your answers, it's important not to memorize them word-for-word; instead, make sure they sound natural and like something you'd say if asked the question in real life.

You should also remember that many of these questions will be basic inquiries about where you went to school and what projects/jobs/internships are relevant to the job opening at hand. Some might be more specific or unusual depending on what position you're applying for (e.g., "If a tree falls in a forest but no one hears it fall, does it make a sound?"). As such, it's good practice to read up on some sample interview questions beforehand so that no matter what situation arises during an interview situation, there won't be any surprises from either side!

Arrive on Time

Arrive on time. This is a simple yet crucial guideline to follow in life. Arriving late will throw off your entire interview and make you look unprofessional. It's best to arrive at least ten minutes early if possible and give yourself enough time to calm down, collect yourself, and get ready before the interview starts.

If this isn't possible for whatever reason (traffic congestion or bad weather), then be sure to call the company beforehand and let them know that you will be late so they can make arrangements for your arrival. If they mention an earlier time slot (for example: "I can offer you 9 am this morning instead of 10 am"), take it! The sooner you arrive at an interview site, the better the chance of getting in and out quickly without running into any issues along the way.

Dress Appropriately for an Interview

You've been invited to an interview, and it's time to get dressed. It's tempting to wear what you wore the last time you interviewed, but that may not be the best idea. Even if the job is similar, there's no guarantee that it will be held in an identical environment or with people who are familiar with your style. The best way to stand out is by dressing professionally and confidently so that hiring managers remember their first impression of you as one of competence and comfort in your skin.

How do I know what kind of clothes make me look confident? Asking yourself some questions can help: If I were offered this job today, would I feel good about how I looked going into work each day? Am I wearing clothing that makes me feel comfortable and confident—not just because my mom said so (or even because my friends told me they liked it), but because it represents who I am? Will these clothes also make me stand out from other candidates for this position?

Listen to the Questions Carefully and Answer Them with Focus

- Listen to the question carefully and give it some thought before you answer.

- Focus on the question and answer it carefully, without worrying about other questions or what you should have said.

Be Prepared to Sell Yourself

Unfortunately, a job interview isn't just about answering questions. You need to be prepared and confident enough in your abilities that you can sell yourself. That means you should prepare to talk about your skills, experience, and achievements throughout the interview process.

You'll also want to be ready with answers to questions about your weaknesses. If they ask you this question during an interview, they may just be trying to gauge how honest of a person you are or if there's anything else they should know about before hiring you. If a potential employer asks why exactly do I want this job? It could mean they are not convinced that interviewing on its own merits would convince them enough. So taking some time off from work might hurt their bottom line if given another opportunity at another company before hiring decisions are made.

Be Positive and Enthusiastic about the Job

As you prepare for an interview, think about how you can best present yourself. Be positive and enthusiastic about the job. It is important to show excitement for both your work and the company. If you are applying for a position in sales, be sure that your enthusiasm is evident when talking about your experience with customers. If you are applying for a role as an accountant, highlight how well-rounded your education has prepared you for this type of work.

Ask Questions About the Job

When it comes to the interview process, there are a few things you should do before your interview and others you should do. The most important is to ask questions about the job, company, and industry. These will help determine if this is somewhere where you want to work. Ask specific questions such as: What will my daily responsibilities be? What kind of training opportunities are there? How much growth potential does this position have? Do they have an internal directory or website where I can see past employee reviews and feedback? The more specific your questions are, the better informed your decision will be.

Different Types of Interviews

Interviews are a great way to get to know someone, but they can be stressful for both parties. Here's how to ace that next job interview and ensure it's a good experience for everyone involved.

An individual interview is the most common, where you meet with a single person or interviewer. It's typically held in a small room with one chair for the candidate and another for the interviewer. The interview time will depend on the employer, but it's usually about 30 minutes long.

You'll typically be asked questions about your experience and qualifications in a one-on-one interview. However, you may also have to answer some situational questions to reveal how well you handle stress, deal with difficult situations, or communicate with others.

Finally, you'll probably be asked if you have any questions. It's important to ask questions in this interview because it shows that you're interested in learning more about the job and the company.

A panel interview consists of two or more people interviewing you at once. It's a popular method used by companies because it can be more efficient and cost-effective than a one-on-one interview, although it can also be intimidating.

Here are some things to keep in mind when preparing for a panel interview:

- Prepare answers that everyone on the panel will find valuable, not just one person.

- Don't try to redirect questions back at one person in particular; this will make you look elusive and difficult to please.

- Remember that the most important thing is whether or not your qualifications meet the company's needs.

- Remember that you're being evaluated by the panel as a whole, not just one person.

- The more you can focus on answering everyone's questions and proving that your qualifications meet the company's needs, the better off you'll be.

Structured Interview

A structured interview is a job interview in which the structure is determined before the interview takes place. The interviewer uses a standard set of questions for all candidates and does not allow them to deviate from their script. Each question asked during this kind of interview has a specific purpose, and candidates are expected to answer each one in a certain way. This can make it difficult for a candidate who isn't familiar with the process, as they may not know what kind of response is expected from them or why they're being asked questions that don't seem relevant to the job.

Structured interviews are most commonly used by large companies hiring many people at once. In this case, a more structured approach can be helpful because it allows the interviewer to ensure they're asking each candidate the same questions and getting them all the same answers. It also helps them identify those candidates who may not be right for the job based on their responses.

Semi-Structured Interview

You may be asked to explain a concept or give an example of a problem you have solved. You may also be asked to describe your approach and how you would solve a problem.

The interviewer will ask about your past experiences, look for evidence of your skills, and assess whether you can articulate a plan for future growth.

It's important to prepare for this interview, as it will likely be your first meeting with the company. The best way to prepare is by researching the company and its products. You should also know about your background to discuss relevant experience or skills.

Telephone Interview

If a company wants to reduce the number of face-to-face interviews, it may ask candidates to have an initial chat over the phone. This is usually the first step in the selection process. Candidates are asked questions about their skills and experience and why they want to work for that company.

Telephone interviews are less expensive than face-to-face interviews because they do not require paying for travel or accommodation expenses for each candidate who will be interviewed. For example, if 100 candidates are interviewed by telephone, only 10% can attend at one time, so you need not worry about your place being crowded with many people at once!

Video Interview

Video interviews are done over the internet; you can use a webcam, cell phone camera, or other video equipment. The interviewer may be in a different country. They will ask you questions, and you will answer them. You can ask questions at the end of your interview.

Peer Group Screening Interview

You may be invited to meet other candidates as part of an informal group discussion or task to see how you can work together.

What Is a Peer Group Screening Interview?

A peer group screening interview is held with a small number of candidates. The interviewer will usually ask you to participate in a small group session, where you will be asked about your skills and experience in the role. You'll then discuss your answers with the other applicants. This type of interview allows employers to see how well you can work with others and whether there's any potential conflict between individuals. It also indicates how well each candidate approaches tasks and challenges presented by work situations.

Outcome-Based Questioning (OBQ) Interviews

In this form of behavioral interviewing, your answers are evaluated using criteria such as competencies like leadership and communication skills rather than technical experience.

This is a good interview technique if you want to hire for management positions or other roles where your candidate will manage others.

It's also useful when there isn't a lot of technical knowledge required in the job description because it focuses on what the candidate can do, not what they know.

Why Knowing What Kind of Interview You're Having Is Important

Knowing what kind of interview you're in for is important because it can help you prepare. For example, if you know that a panel interview is coming up and you aren't used to presenting yourself in front of a group, it's a good idea to practice answering questions out loud so that you don't get caught off guard by their format. It's also beneficial to research the company and job description beforehand. If an employer sends out information about themselves via email, read through it so that when they ask about specific details during the interview process (like what makes them different from other companies), you'll be able to answer confidently without having done anything else besides reading their website!

This is a lot of information, but we hope it helps you prepare for your next interview. Whether a single individual or a panel, the most important thing is to be yourself and be prepared! There are many different types of interviews, but they all have one thing in common—they want to know what makes you tick as an employee and potential colleague. So make sure you go into any interview with confidence in yourself and others around you who support your candidacy. It will help ensure everyone feels good about their decision when making an offer!

Phases of an Interview

Interviews are an essential part of the hiring process. Through it, you can find out more about a candidate and ensure they're a good fit for your company. It also helps you assess whether or not they can do the job well and determine if there are any gaps in their knowledge (which might cause problems down the road).

Behavioral Interview

A behavioral interview is a type of job interview that focuses on past experiences and actions. The interviewer asks the candidate to describe specific situations that require problem-solving or interpersonal skills. It's important to practice how you would answer these questions so you can be prepared for them during the actual interview.

To give an example, here's an example question: "Describe a time when you had to deal with a difficult customer."

The best way to answer this question is by describing how you were able to diffuse the situation and maintain positive relationships. The interviewer wants to know how you handled yourself in both professional and social situations, so include details about how other people responded. (for example: "The customer was upset because she thought our products weren't good quality") as well as any outcomes or consequences of your actions. For example: "She left happy but told everyone at her office not to shop there anymore."

Technical Interview

Technical interview. At this stage, you're being assessed to see if you have the technical skills required for the role. The interviewer will ask about your experience and knowledge of specific technologies and software programs. You must prepare for a technical interview by practicing with a friend or colleague who has experience in the field in which you want to work.

If possible, find out what kind of technology or programming language will be used in your new job before going into an interview. You don't want to get caught off guard when faced with questions on topics that are unfamiliar to you!

Q/A Time

This is a good time for the interviewee to ask questions they have.

Q/A time is a chance for the interviewee to ask questions—but only if they're thoughtful and relevant. It's also an opportunity for you, as the interviewer, to gauge how comfortable they are with this type of conversation. If they ask something that feels invasive or imbalanced in terms of what you've asked them so far, take note! If their questions seem superficial or too broad (e.g., "What are your hours like?"), keep an eye out for that as well! Likewise, if their questions seem negative ("Do I need this job?"). Consider steering them back toward more positive territory by asking follow-up questions: "What were you hoping would happen at this stage?" or "How do we get there?"

Executive Summary

Creating an Executive Summary

The executive summary is the first thing any interviewer sees when they open your resume. It's your opportunity to make a compelling case for why you're the best candidate for the job, so it must represent all of your skills and experience in a concise way.

To create an executive summary, break down each key data point from your resume into three to five bullet points that showcase what makes you unique. Here are some examples:

- "Extensive experience with word processing software (MS Word)." - This shows that you have knowledge of document formatting tools but don't specify what documents were edited or how much time was spent doing so.

- "Managed team of five associates across two offices." - This indicates leadership experience but doesn't show whether or not this person had much interaction with clients or other departments within their organization (or even outside).

Research Interview

A research interview is a conversation between you and the client to learn more about their needs, expectations, and goals. This interview phase aims to better understand what your client wants to accomplish with this project. You can use this information to help determine if they're ready for an MVP or if they need more internal support before moving forward with building anything.

To conduct your research interviews:

- Find out who will be involved in the development process (the team). Get their contact info so you can reach out once you have all your materials together for each phase of the interview process.

- Next, determine who will be affected by what you're building (stakeholders). These people are interested in seeing something built that addresses their professional needs or improves upon them somehow. For example, management might want better sales data from its current system to make better hiring practices and marketing campaign decisions. Engineers could benefit from having a new dashboard feature on their computers that gives them faster access to information. Designers would love having easy access via mobile devices like tablets/smartphones so they could collaborate with fellow teammates around town while away from their desks during off hours like weekends when everyone else isn't there yet (or go home early).

Analysis

This is where you are going to start making sense of your data.

You will use it to identify trends and patterns, find correlations and relationships between variables, and determine what is important and what is not.

Synthesis and Design

This is where you create your final product. You will first synthesize your ideas and design a product that meets those requirements.

Prototype

The prototype is the model of your design. It can be physical or digital, but it's usually a little bit of both. The prototype can be used to test your design with users and stakeholders before you start coding. It also helps set expectations for developers and other stakeholders by clarifying what they'll have to build and how they should do it—no surprises!

In some cases, prototypes are created using coding tools like HTML5 canvas or JavaScript libraries like jQuery; in others, they're more like storyboards that show people what your product will look like through sketches or mockups (like this sketchy-looking one). Either way, prototypes give people an idea of what the final version will look like so that everyone's on board with how things will work from the get-go.

Test and Refine

Testing is a crucial part of the design process. It involves getting feedback on your design and testing to determine if it works as expected. Testing, especially usability testing, can also help ensure that your product meets user needs and wants.

Some of These Steps May Only Be a Few Days Each, and Others May Take Much Longer

Some steps are more important than others, and some are more difficult.

Let's talk about what to expect during the interview so you can fully prepare for every step of your next big job opportunity!

At the end of this process, you should have a pretty good idea of whether or not someone is right for the job. If they're not quite ready yet, they may be able to come back later with more experience under their belt and try again!

Chapter 2

Different Programming Languages

Programming languages are the foundation of what we do as developers. They're the building blocks of software, and they've evolved to suit our changing needs better. Different programming languages have different strengths, weaknesses, requirements, and purposes. Some are meant for specific applications, while others are designed to be universal in scope. By learning a few different programming languages, you'll be able to choose which is right for any given project or situation!

C

C is a general-purpose programming language that's been around for decades. It's the most popular programming language in the world, and it's used to build many different things—from operating systems to cellular phones. However, when people talk about C, they usually refer to "C89," released in 1989 as an update on C86 (also known as ANSI C).

C89 added many new features that made it possible for programmers to write more complicated programs than ever before:

things like function prototypes, inline assembly code blocks, compound literals (or "declaration lists"), variadic macros with ellipses in their parameter lists... these were all part of what made C89 such an improvement over its predecessor.

Palindrome Numbers In C

Palindromes are numbers or expressions that read the same way, forward or backward. For example, 101, 102, and 666 are palindromic. Every non-empty English word with at least one letter is a palindrome. But what about numbers? Are there any integers that are palindromes? If so, how do we recognize them?

What Are Palindrome Numbers?

Palindromic numbers are also called pangrams. A palindrome is a number that is the same when its digits are reversed.

Example: 54670 = 5467 5050

The first one is the reverse of 54675050, and it has no palindrome numbers, whereas the second one has only one palindrome number, 5050, because it can be split into two equal parts, and each part will still produce a valid string when reversed: 50 500

How to Recognize Palindromes?

A number is palindromic if it reads the same forwards and backward. The same number can be written in different ways. For example, 123 can be written as 321, 321, or 1231.

The function of this program is to find all the palindromic numbers which are less than 10 million and print them on the screen.

How to Recognize Non-Palindromes

A number is a palindrome if it is equal to its reverse.

For example, 54321, 78901, 11234, and 12343 are palindromes. But 12345 is not a palindrome because it's not equal to 94531 (reverse).

Program to Check Whether a Given Number Is Palindrome

To check if a given number is Palindrome, we will use the fact that it is easy to reverse any string character by character. So, for example, if we have a string "abcdefg" and want to reverse it, then we just need to write each character of the alphabet from "d" to "a" from right to left.

Now let us see how this works for an integer:

Let us say we are given an integer 123456 and want to check whether it is Palindrome or not. We first convert it into its corresponding string, which will be "123456," and then reverse that string (from right to left), which gives us 678453 as the reversed form of our input number, 123456. Now, if we compare these two strings, they do not match because three characters differ between them, i.e., 1st and 2nd digits of the original string and 5th and 4th digits of reversed counterpart. Therefore there exists no possibility of reversing an integer into itself, so our program should return false otherwise, true.

C++ is a high-level language that's used to create applications and programs. It uses curly brackets to define blocks of code and supports procedural, object-oriented, and generic programming. C++ is primarily used in systems development, although it can also be used for developing mobile apps and video games. The language has many features that allow you to write complex programs efficiently but still offers flexibility when developing large projects.

Why Use C++?

You may be wondering why you should use C++ rather than another language. C++ is a general-purpose programming language that can be used to develop any type of application. It is also an object-oriented language, which uses classes to organize code and data, making it easier to manage larger projects. Additionally, C++ is a compiled language that runs directly on your computer's hardware instead of in an interpreted environment like Java (which would require extra processing time). This makes it run faster than other languages, such as JavaScript or Python. Finally, since C++ is a low-level programming language, you have direct access to the machine's resources for maximum performance and efficiency when running your programs.

Who Uses C++?

As a general-purpose programming language, C++ can be used to create applications, drivers, and operating systems. It's also popular among game developers thanks to its close ties with OpenGL, the standard API for writing 2D and 3D graphics.

C++ is a common choice in computer science and engineering because it highly controls memory management and other system resources. C++ programmers can access low-level operations through the standard library, but they can choose not to use those features if they don't need them.

Finally, C++ has become increasingly popular as an implementation language for high-performance computing (HPC) projects due to its excellent performance on massively parallel computers such as GPUs.

What Is a High-Level Language?

A high-level language is a programming language that offers more abstraction than an assembly language or machine code. High-level languages are easier to use, learn, read and maintain. Anyone can read a high-level program; you don't have to be an expert in computer science to understand what a program does when written in C++. There are many advantages of using high-level languages over the assembly or machine code:

- They are easier to read

- They produce smaller programs.

- The compiler can perform many checks on the code before it is executed (for example, memory allocation errors)

Getting Started with C++

To start programming in C++, you must install the compiler and IDE. You can download the free Visual Studio Community edition from Microsoft's website.

Once you have installed Visual Studio, you can create a new project and add a source file. A source file is a text file containing your program's code. In addition, the IDE will automatically generate a function called main() that runs when you run or compile your program; this function contains all of the statements that will execute when someone runs (or compiles) your program.

Variables and Constants

Variables and constants are identifiers that identify objects in the program. They can be thought of as names for values. Variables can change their value during execution, whereas constants hold a fixed value throughout the execution of a program.

The following are some important concepts related to variables:

Declaring variables: You declare a variable with its type name before using it in your code. For example, you may have declared an integer variable named x with int x; or a character array named string[] by using char[].

The general syntax for declaring a variable is as follows:

    type variable_name;

Here's an example:

    int age; char name[50]; * Initializing variables:

It is necessary to initialize all global variables before use (otherwise, they will remain uninitialized). Here's an example where we initialize our age and first_name arrays:

    int age = 20; char first_name[]={'J', 'u', 's', 't', 'i', 'n'};
    String lastName = "Marks"; String title="Manager"; String
    role="Team Leader".

Data Types in C++

The types of data that you can store in a variable are called data types. There are several types of data available in C++. Here's a list:

- **int**: Integer values (whole numbers) with no fractional part

- **Float**: Real floating-point values that have either an integer or decimal value (divisible by 10 without any remainder)

- **Double**: Real floating-point values that have either an integer or decimal value (divisible by 10 without any remainder)

- **char**: Character values ranging from 0 to 255

Strings in C++

The std::string class represents C++ strings.

You can concatenate strings using the + operator.

> Strings can be compared with == or != operators, but don't forget to use std::to_string()!

Operators in C++

Operators are symbols that perform calculations between operands. Operators can be categorized as arithmetic, bitwise (binary), logical, or assignment.

- **Arithmetic Operators**: +, -, * and /

- **Bitwise Operators**: ~ (one's complement), | (or), & (and) (and =)

- **Logical Operators**: !(not), && (and), ||(or).

- **Assignment Operator**: = += -= *= /= %= ^= **= ~~ > >>> ~~~ +

Implementing a Class or Member Function in C++

You can define a class and its member functions in one place, or you can define them separately.

If you want to define a class and its member functions in one place, use the following syntax:

    class MyClassName { // Class definition goes here. } // End of class definition.

To implement a member function within this class, use the following syntax:

    void MyClassName::FunctionName() { // Function implementation goes here. }// End of function implementation.

To define a class and its member functions separately, use the following syntax:

    class MyClassName { // Class definition goes here. };// End of the class definition. void MyClassName::FunctionName()

{ // Function implementation goes here. }// End of function implementation.

Analyzing C++ Code Execution

The Visual Studio debugger is a powerful and useful tool that can help you understand how your program executes, and it's built into the IDE. You can use it to step through code one line at a time, set breakpoints (places where execution will pause), view variables values in memory, evaluate expressions, and more.

You can also profile your code to see what functions are taking up most of the execution time (and which ones aren't being called at all). This is useful for optimizing performance when working with large projects that use many libraries.

The memory analyzer helps you find memory leaks—where objects are no longer used but still reside in memory because they're referenced by another object or variable that hasn't been destroyed yet. This could eventually lead to fragmentation issues in large projects, so once you've found them using this tool, fix them!

If any part of your code doesn't seem right or doesn't behave as expected, then use its Code Analyzer feature.

Assignment Operator

The assignment operator is a binary operator that assigns values to variables. The assignment operator is a member function, meaning it's part of the class definition. It has the same name as the object it operates on, followed by an equal sign (=).

Assignment operators have three basic properties:

- Assignment operators assign values to variables.

- Assignment operators can be used in expressions and statements.

- Assignment operators are used to initialize variables and change their value at runtime (as opposed to compile time).

Python

Python is a general-purpose programming language used to create web applications and perform data analysis and artificial intelligence tasks. Python is also used in game development and scientific computing.

Python has a large following among students due to its clear syntax, which helps beginners learn the language quickly. It's also popular among professionals because of its flexibility: Python can be used for small one-off scripts and large programs that handle massive amounts of data.

The ease with which Python can be picked up by people new to programming makes it an ideal first language for beginners; however, Python has been around long enough to acquire some complexity on its own merits as well.

Java

Java is a general-purpose, object-oriented programming language. Sun Microsystems originally developed it in the early 1990s to run on any operating system that supports the Java Virtual Machine (JVM), including Windows, macOS, and Linux. The language has a significantly simpler object model and fewer low-level capabilities than C++.

Bytecode generated by compiling a Java application can run on any JVM, regardless of the computer architecture.

This enables portability for the software running on it and makes it easier for multiple platforms to use them simultaneously without affecting each other in most cases (except when using native methods). As of 2015, Java is one of the most popular programming languages used, particularly for client-server web applications or mobile app development when supported by a virtual machine such as Oracle's HotSpot Client VM or IBM's J9 VM. Unfortunately, many servers also run their proprietary versions, such as Apache Tomcat & IBM Websphere Application Server, etc., and other embedded devices like wireless phones or set-top boxes. These may not support virtualization technologies but require backward compatibility with existing systems already deployed elsewhere over time (see Porting#Migration_from_analogue_to_digital).

The Java Programming language is a general-purpose computer programming language. It is used to write apps on desktops, laptops, mobile phones, and many other devices.

Keywords

Java keywords are words that have special meaning to the Java compiler. They're case-sensitive, so using them in lowercase or camel case is not valid. The following table lists keywords used in Java 8:

- assert

- break

- byte

- case

- catch

- char (Java 5+)

Data Containers

There are many data types in Java, and they can be divided into two categories: primitive and reference. Primitive data types are basic data types like int, float, and char. Reference data types store the memory address where an object is stored in memory (like an array or collection).

Thread Scheduler

Java is a concurrent programming language used to write programs that execute in multiple threads simultaneously.

Classes are the fundamental building blocks of a Java program. A class defines an object with its variables (fields) and methods. Classes also define what happens when you create an instance of that class, including initializing its fields and assigning values to them.

Java is an object-oriented programming language, which means that you store data in objects instead of storing it as simple values or plain text. An object is a logical grouping of related data and code. It can be manipulated through any access point (an action) by calling on methods attached to the object or other objects contained within it. This way, an entire collection of information related to one topic or subject can be bundled into one logical thing called "an object."

Java Has Become One of the Most Popular Programming Languages Ever Created

Java is a programming language and computing platform. It's used for developing applications and programs, including Android apps. Sun Microsystems developed Java in the 1990s, which later sold it to Oracle Corporation (formerly known as Sun Microsystems).

Java is a general-purpose, high-level programming language that can be used to create a wide variety of different types of software programs. These include server-side web applications (i.e., those that run on web servers), utilities such as games, desktop GUI applications (i.e., those with a graphical user interface), mobile apps (i.e., those running on smartphones), embedded systems firmware, and more!

JavaScript

JavaScript is one of the most popular programming languages today. It was created in 1995 by Brendan Eich and was initially used in Netscape Navigator 2.0. JavaScript is a scripting language, and it can be run directly on the client side or server-side as well as inside web browsers.

JavaScript specifies several data types, such as strings, numbers, Booleans, null values, and arrays (lists).

JavaScript can be used for many things: Client-side scripting - running scripts locally to provide functionality like adding/removing elements from HTML pages; Server-side scripting - running scripts on a server using NodeJS or another framework; Mobile programming - writing apps for smartphones and tablets; Desktop application development - developing desktop applications like Adobe Photoshop or Microsoft Office products.

R

R is a programming language and software environment for statistical computing and graphics. It is an implementation of the S language (a versatile, high-level programming language that provides all the basic features needed for numerical computation and data analysis), a dialect of S-PLUS. The core team comprises a dozen full-time developers and about two dozen part-time developers working on R full-time. R expresses the latest information on the research being done in the global scientific community that enables us to predict the future.

R is an open-source software project originating at The r Foundation for Statistical Computing with contributions from many worldwide individuals.

Swift

Swift is a programming language developed by Apple Inc. for iOS, macOS, watchOS, tvOS, and Linux. It was introduced in 2014 as a replacement for Objective-C and C++. The Swift programming language has proved to be a major success with developers who work on the iPhone and iPad platforms. This popularity is replicated across other platforms such as macOS and Apple TV.

Swift is designed to be more efficient than Objective-C or C++ by providing features such as closures (programming constructs), tuples (data structures), or optional (optional variables).

Scala

Scala is a general-purpose programming language designed to express common programming patterns concisely, elegantly, and type-safely. It smoothly integrates features of object-oriented and functional languages. In addition, Scala is used for server-side development for companies like Twitter, LinkedIn, and Foursquare.

Scala is also an object-oriented language with functional paradigms like pattern matching and higher-order functions. This makes it possible to simultaneously use all OOPs and FP paradigms' benefits!

The Scala programming language is a powerful and flexible tool for any programming job. Whether you're working on back-end applications, high-concurrency web apps, desktop clients, or scalable data service clusters, Scala will help you write cleaner, more effective code.

Kotlin

Kotlin (pronounced "coterminal," or simply Kotlin) is a statically-typed programming language that targets the Java Virtual Machine (JVM), JavaScript, and Android. Kotlin is designed to be a practical refinement of Java and follows the style of Scala.

It's a modern, open-source, statically typed programming language for the JVM, Android, and the browser. Kotlin offers all benefits of OOP: strong typing, interfaces, abstraction, etc., but it also has features like null safety (no more NullPointerExceptions), extension functions, and smart casts. In addition, it's fully interoperable with Java, so you can use any existing Java frameworks or libraries in your Kotlin code.

Go, Lang

Go Lang is a general-purpose programming language developed in 2007 by Google. Go Lang was designed to be an alternative to C++, which can be difficult to learn and use.

Go Lang is used for web development, but it's also used for other applications such as robotics and even low-level systems programming. Go Lang is statically typed, meaning variables must be declared before they can be used. It also has type inference, where the language can figure out what type of variable should be based on its context; if it doesn't know what data you want it to hold, then your program will not compile!

Perl 6

Perl 6 is a Perl-based, multi-paradigm, object-oriented language. It's the most popular programming language in the world, and it's also known as "the duct tape of the Internet."

Perl 6 was designed to fill in some of Perl 5's gaps and fix its flaws. For example, it has:

- A cleaner syntax than its predecessor with fewer curly brackets

- More detailed documentation that makes it easy for beginners to learn

These Are the Most Popular Programming Languages

- **C** is the oldest programming language, originally developed in 1972. It's used to write complex systems and is still widely used today.

- **Python** is a general-purpose programming language introduced in 1991 and has become increasingly popular. It was designed with readability, so it's easy to pick up if you're new to coding, and it has been translated into hundreds of different languages.

- **Java** is also a general-purpose programming language but with more specific uses than Python—it was built for supporting app development on mobile phones (Android), desktops (J2SE), and web browsers (JavaScript).

- **JavaScript** has been around since 1995 when Netscape Navigator 2 included the first version of it as part of its browser technology called Navigator LiveScript. Later renamed JScript, then finally JavaScript after Netscape acquired Sun Microsystems, which had developed Java before being acquired by Oracle Corporation. Today HTML5 supports most features from ES6/ECMAScript 6, which are backward compatible. So there's no need for transpilers like Babel anymore. Except if you want them enabled anyway due to personal preference reasons like developers who work on open source software projects. Here they need these tools available locally without having access to online resources at their disposal all day long during work hours.

Chapter 3

Different Types of Data Structures

Data structures provide a way to organize data. They allow us to store and retrieve information efficiently, which is important when working with large datasets. Like the tools you might use in the real world (such as hammers, saws, and screwdrivers), many different types of data structures can be used for different purposes.

Array

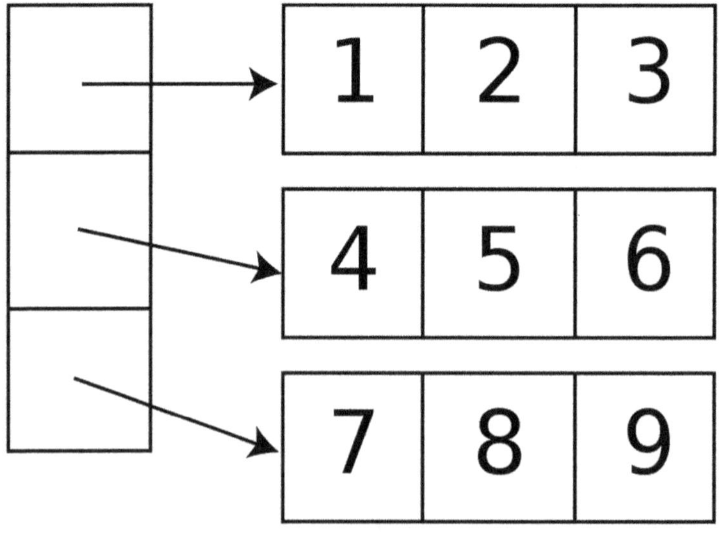

An array is a collection of elements. It is an ordered list of data, and the elements in arrays are homogeneous. The size of arrays can be fixed or dynamic. Arrays are one of the most used data structures in programming languages because they are easy to implement and use, which makes them ideal for application programming interfaces (APIs) that need to work with large amounts of data.

A fixed-size array is a sequential collection of elements with contiguous memory locations allocated at compile time. In C++, these variables will be allocated on the stack rather than on the heap, like other objects would be if they were created using a new operator instead. Fixed-size arrays are faster than dynamic ones because they don't require any extra memory allocations during runtime (elements can be accessed directly without having to allocate any additional space), but this comes at a cost. You cannot add new elements once your original array has reached its capacity limit (which means you will have wasted some memory).

Duplication in an Array

Duplication In An Array is a popular problem first proposed by D.E. Knuth and R.L. Miller in 1973. The problem is to find any number that occurs more than once in an array of numbers.

Approach 1: Optimized Solution

This is the easiest solution, but it doesn't consider that each value could occur multiple times in one string.

Here's what you do:

- Store the values of your array in a HashMap (if you don't know what this is, read up).

- Store the number of occurrences for each value in another HashMap. This will be used to find duplicates later on! If a number is found more than once, this string occurs multiple times with different values, so we can use that information when tallying how many times each item occurs in our final data structure (see step 4).

- Finally, store indexes corresponding to where these items appear within your original array using their unique name as an identifier (instead of their actual value).

- Now, all we have left is to loop through every single item and add its count and index into our new data structure based on what was stored earlier!

- The result of this algorithm is a data structure containing the number of occurrences for each value in your array. This can be used to find later duplicates (e.g., if you're trying to calculate word frequencies).

Approach 2: Brute Force Solution

This approach is also known as the brute force solution. It's named after the computer science term "brute force," which means "to solve a problem by trying every possible answer until you find one that works."

This approach works because it tries all possible duplicates and returns True if any of them are found or False if none are found.

As in Approach 1, this code loops through the array. However, instead of searching for two elements that have exactly equal values and comparing their locations, this code simply compares each item with itself:

```python
for i in range(0, len(array)):

if array[i] == array[i]:

return True
```

This approach is more efficient than Approach 1 because it doesn't need to loop through the entire array. Instead, it only needs to compare each item with itself. This means there can be fewer comparisons overall, which will speed up your code.

This Will Be a New Variant of the Popular Problem - Find a Duplicate in an Array

First, let's think about why we even want to do this. We have an array of items that we want to check for duplicates. So how do we get our hands on the array? The first approach is by using a list comprehension:

```python
```python

def duplicates(arr):

return [x for x in arr if x not in set(arr)][0]
```
```

The second approach is with a generator:

```python
def duplicates(arr): return list(set(arr) & set(arr))
```

The third approach is with a generator expression:

```python
def duplicates(arr): return (set(arr) & set(arr))
```

The fourth and final approach is with a list comprehension:

```python
def duplicates(arr): return [x for x in arr if x not in set(arr)]
```

The generator expression is often the preferred approach. It can be used as an alternative to listing comprehensions with a single yield statement inside it.

Matrix

$$\begin{bmatrix} 1 & 0 & 0 \\ 0 & 1 & 0 \\ 0 & 0 & 1 \end{bmatrix}$$

A matrix is a rectangular array of numbers. Matrices are useful for solving linear equations and analyzing and representing transformations in geometry.

Matrix dimensions can be 2-D or 3-D. The number of rows (denoted by m) is called the width, and the number of columns (denoted by n) is called the height. A matrix with m rows and n columns is known as an m × n matrix; it is usually written as "M" or "M." For example, a 3 × 2 matrix would have three rows and two columns: you can think of it as an Excel spreadsheet where you have three rows with two columns in each row (i.e., 3 × 2).

Linked List

A linked list is a data structure where each element is connected to the next in a chain. A linked list can be used to store items of different types, such as integers or strings.

Linked lists are easy to add or remove elements from the beginning or end of the list (the "head" and "tail"), but adding an element at some other position requires traversing the entire list until you reach that point.

A Linked List Is a Collection of Nodes

A linked list is a collection of nodes. Each node contains a piece of data and a pointer to the next node in the list. In this way, nodes are connected. The first node is called the head, while any other node that isn't at either end of the list is called a tail.

The head and tail may not be at opposite ends of the list. For example, if you were to create an ordered list (a type of linked list), you might want your first item to be at position zero instead of position one so that it appears before all others when displayed on the screen or printed out as text.

Each Node Points to the Next Element in the List

- Nodes are the basic building block of linked lists. They contain data and a link to the next node in the list.

- The word node is often used because nodes are like the nodes of a tree.

- Nodes can be linked together in any order and form any structure for storing data (e.g., sorted or unsorted).

The First Node in the List Is Called the Head. The Last Node in the List Is Called the Tail

The first node in the list is called the head. The last node in the list is called the tail. Nodes are always added to, or removed from, these two parts of a linked list, not anywhere else. This means that they are always together and they have a special relationship with each other.

Nodes may also be called nodes because they're points where data can be accessed in a graph structure or network!

Nodes Can Be Dynamically Allocated and Deallocated

Dynamic memory allocation is a technique for managing memory in which the memory for a variable can be assigned or reassigned during program execution.

There Is No Limit on How Long a Linked List Can Be

- It is possible to have a very long linked list.

- The only limit is the amount of memory in your computer.

Linked lists are data structures that consist of a chain of nodes. These nodes contain both data items and pointers to the next node in the list. Linked lists allow elements to be added or removed from the end or middle of the list in constant time and access to any element in constant time (O(1)).

Each node has two parts: one for storing its value and another for referencing other nodes in the list; this reference is called its link. As we navigate through our list, we start at the first element (the head) and then move downwards until we reach its tail element (also known as "tail").

Each time you encounter an entry whose key doesn't match yours, you check whether it points directly to another key with which it shares part of its hashcode (i.e., if their keys differ by only one character). If so, you can continue there instead of starting over from scratch by checking whether your new friend's key matches yours more closely than any other possible entry. Then you continue downwards with your newly found friend until reaching another mismatch or hitting bottom. Where no matching entries were found either way yet so far due to lack thereof being present within that particular iteration around, said tree structure, upon reaching the bottom branches next up, would lead us back to where we originally started. But since they weren't part 1st time around either since they weren't part 2nd time around either since they weren't part.

Sort Lists

You may have noticed that some of the lists in this tutorial are sorted, and others are not sorted. The reason for this is that sorting lists are easy!

If your list has an even number of items, it should be sorted using a bubble sort algorithm. If your list has an odd number of items, use a merge sort algorithm instead.

To use the bubble sort algorithm:

- Start with any item in your list as the first item in your new list (which will then be empty).

- Compare this first item to each subsequent item in turn and swap it if they are out of order (i.e., smaller than bigger or vice versa).

- Repeat these steps until you reach the end of the list without making any swaps (meaning all items are present in the correct order).

Loop in List

To sort a linked list, you'll need to change the order of its elements by swapping them around. There are two ways to swap two nodes: through their pointers or by moving both of them over one spot (with no change to either pointer). The first method is faster but more complicated; the second method is simpler but slower.

The simplest way to sort an unordered array (like what you'd get with []) involves creating an auxiliary array that holds random numbers between 0 and N-1 (where N is how many items there are in your original array). You then use these randomly selected numbers as indices into your original array, swapping whatever element happens to be at those indices. The result will be completely randomized. This makes sense if you think about it—since nothing keeps this process from happening simultaneously instead of one element at a time!

Stack

A stack is a last-in, first-out (LIFO) data structure. It is used to store data in the form of variables and objects. A stack can be similar to a stack of plates or other objects where you must put items on top of each other and take them off from the bottom one at a time.

Stacks are linear data structures because they can only contain one layer of information. Therefore, the only way for an item on a stack to move up or down is by pushing it onto another stack with more data storage space.

Queue

A queue is a linear data structure that maintains order. Items are added to the end of the queue and removed from the front of it. The first item to enter a queue (enqueue) is the first to exit (dequeue).

You can think about a queue as an assembly line for manufacturing cars: workers bring parts one at a time down an assembly line until all those parts have been added to cars. The same goes for our queues: items come in through one side and go out through another, automatically keeping everything neat!

There are two main operations for any kind of data structure: enqueue and dequeue. Enqueuing means adding something to its back end; dequeuing means removing something from its front end.

Stack: Push and Pop

The Stack class provides the following methods:

- **push():** appends an element to the top of the stack

- **pop():** removes and returns an element from the top of the stack (does not change its size)

- **top():** returns but does not remove the last element added to this stack

Stack - Top, isEmpty, and Size

The Stack class allows you to access its top element with the top() method and check whether it's empty with isEmpty(). You can also obtain a count of the number of elements in a stack by calling size().

Queue - Enqueue and Dequeue

You can add an item to the end of a queue by using the enqueue method:

```
queue.enqueue(1)
```

You can also remove an item from the front of a queue using dequeue:

```
item = queue.dequeue()
```

Queue – qTop, isEmpty, Size and Sort

- **qTop** - returns the element of the queue

- **isEmpty** - returns True if the queue is empty

- **size** - returns the number of elements in the queue

- **sort** - sorts the elements in the queue

Learn How to Use Stack and Queue with Python

A stack is a data structure that can be used to implement recursion. A queue is also a data structure, but unlike stacks, queues are linear.

Both structures can be implemented using linked lists or arrays. They play important roles in computer science and many other fields, such as data mining, machine learning, and artificial intelligence (AI). In Python, there is first-class support for both of these structures, making it easy for developers to use them in their applications.

This is a very common data structure in computer science and is used in many applications. Therefore, it is important to know how to use this data structure so that you can understand more complicated programs.

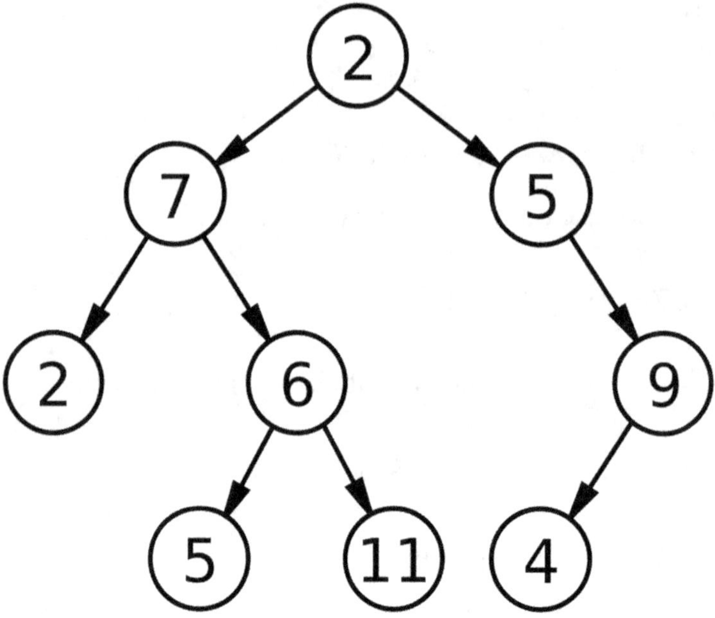

A tree is a data structure that contains nodes and connects them. The connections between nodes form a directed acyclic graph (DAG). A DAG is a unidirectional graph with no cycles.

A tree has a root node, and all other nodes are connected to the root node. Each node in the tree has zero or more children but never both. So, for example, you can't have two "b" s as children of each other because then there would be a cycle in your DAG—you'd have b->b->b->b->b->…, which is not allowed!

Next Nodes in Binary Trees

Finding the next nodes in a binary tree is a classic computer science problem.

What Is It?

The next node is a node in a binary tree connected to the current node through a link. The next node also serves as the successor of the current node, which means it will be your next step if you are exploring from start to finish.

Why Does It Matter?

When it comes to data structures, binary trees are one of the most commonly used ones. They have many applications, from representing hierarchical data (such as filesystems) to implementing practical algorithms such as sorting, searching, and graph traversal. For example, every time you use Google Maps on your phone, you use a binary tree (or something similar).

How to Solve It?

In this problem, you will use recursion to solve the puzzle. The first thing to do is set up a stack or queue (an array). Then, you need to track how many nodes are in each row and column. You can do this by adding 1 for each node added. Once this is done, you can start populating the grid using recursion and your previously initialized stack/queue.

This solution is not very efficient because it uses a lot of memory. If you have a large puzzle, the stack/queue may run out of room before the program finishes. This can be remedied by using heap memory instead of stack memory, but that's beyond the scope of this book.

The second way to solve this problem is by using the Fibonacci sequence. You can do this in two ways:

1. You can use recursion to solve the puzzle and then calculate each row and column based on the value of the numbers in that row and column.

2. Use a dynamic programming approach to calculate each row/column by first calculating the values for each sub-section of that row/column.

The Fibonacci sequence is a sequence with the following property: For any positive integer n, the Fibonacci sequence F_n contains the sum of the two preceding elements in that array.

Binary Search Tree Verification

Binary search trees are used in many data structures. They're especially useful when you need to look up something quickly, like a phone book or a dictionary.

Checking for Binary Search

Let's say you've got a binary search tree and want to check whether it's balanced.

First, what do we mean by "balanced"? We mean that each node's left child has a value less than or equal to its parent's value, and likewise for the right child. If this is not true at any point in your tree, then your tree is unbalanced. Let's look at an example:

Suppose you have a binary search tree with the following values: 4, 8, 9, and 11. This is an unbalanced tree because node 5 has a value of 9, which is greater than its parent (node 3).

Keys Are Unique

Binary Search Trees are built such that each node should contain only one key. You have a linked list if there is more than one key in a node. This means that the BST is no longer what it's supposed to be since there is now an order between the elements, and it might not be efficient anymore.

If you want to keep your binary search tree as efficient as possible, ensure that every key will only be contained in one node!

A Node with Left Subtree

Nodes to the left of a given node always have smaller key values. For example, consider the following binary search tree:

Notice that the left subtree only contains nodes with keys less than or equal to 2 (the key of the root node). To check whether this is true for every node in your BST, you can use recursion as follows:

```
def check_left_subtree(BST):
```

If you have a BST that contains 1,000 nodes and check the left subtree of each node, this will take approximately 1,000,000 operations. On the other hand, if you have a BST with just 100 nodes (which is still pretty big), it will take 10 million operations!

A Node with Right Subtree

You can verify the binary search tree property by checking whether the following conditions are met:

- Only nodes with keys that are greater than or equal to the node's key are included in the right subtree of a node.

- The node should have bigger keys than it's left subtree.

- At least one of the left or right subtrees must be a binary search tree (because if it isn't, it can't have any keys greater than its parent).

The Binary Search Trees

The left and right subtrees are part of the same binary search tree. If they weren't both binary search trees themselves, then we wouldn't have a valid BST!

If we were in a position where either one of them wasn't a BST, our original BST would be invalid, too, because it's impossible to have two non-BSTs connected into one single object!

So if you want to check whether or not your tree is correct (and therefore be able to add nodes), then these two parts need to be valid too.

A Binary Search Tree Is a Data Structure That Allows Us to Locate Something Quickly in a Sorted List

Keys label the nodes of the binary search tree. The keys can be any values, but usually, they're integers or strings. Nodes with larger values than their children are called internal nodes; nodes with smaller values are called leaf nodes.

Graphs

Graphs are a collection of nodes and edges. Nodes are points, while edges are lines that connect nodes. In a graph, the nodes can have properties (like age or weight), while each edge also has properties (like length). Graphs come in two flavors:

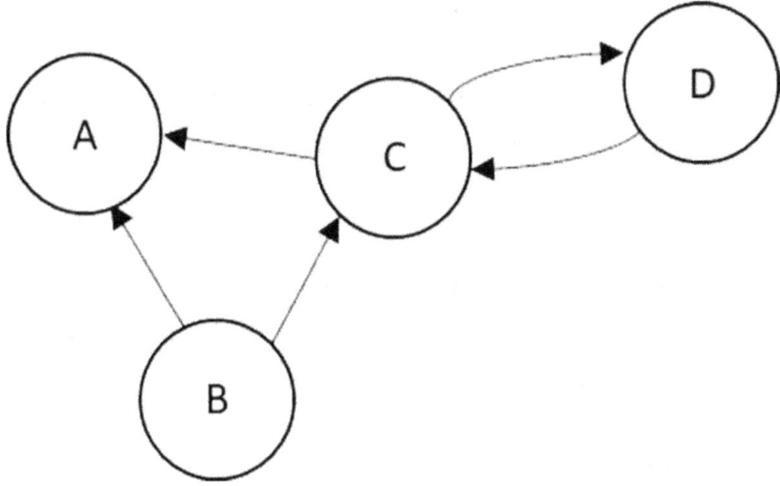

A directed graph is one in which all relationships between the nodes are one-way arrows—you can only follow an arrow from one node to another, but not vice versa.

An undirected graph is just like a regular graph, except that there aren't any directional relationships between the nodes.

Hash Tables

Hash tables are an example of a data structure that stores information in a very efficient manner. A hash table is a type of associative array, which means it maps keys to values. Hash tables are used to store many different types of data and have many applications, including:

- Storing language-specific representations for words and phrases

- Storing the number of times a keyword appears on web pages on search engines such as Google or Bing

- Storing file names based on their content (e.g., pictures versus documents)

Strings in Coding

String handling is a fundamental part of any programming language. In this article, we'll explore how strings work and how you can use them in coding.

Strings in JavaScript

Strings are used to store text. They are immutable, so they cannot be changed after they are created. Strings can be concatenated by placing them next to each other (e.g., "Hello" + "World").

Creating Strings with Quotes in JavaScript

You use double quotes to create a string literal. String literals are sequences of text in which you can embed escape sequences for special characters. For example, if you want to express the phrase "coding is fun" with backslash (\) as an escape sequence, then you should use single quotes:

```javascript

let codeIsFun = 'coding is fun';
```

Conversely, if you want to express the phrase "coding is fun" with backslash as an escape sequence, then you should use double quotes:

```
javascript let codeIsFun = 'coding is
fun';
```

The following escape sequences are available in JavaScript: \\ - Backslash (\) itself. Use this if you want to embed a backslash in your string literal. \' - Single quote (') itself. Use this if you want to embed a single quote in your string literal. \" - Double quote (") itself. Use this if you want to embed a literal double quote in your string. \b - Backspace character (control+H). \f - Form feed character (control+L).

Concatenation in JavaScript

Concatenation is the process of appending one string to another. In JavaScript, concatenation is done using the plus sign (+). For example:

```
var message = "Hello " + "World!";
```

This code creates a variable named message that contains these words: Hello, World! If you want to create a string like this and don't care about its length, then you can use single quotes instead of double quotes:

```
var str = 'Hello ' + 'World!';
```

The plus sign is used to concatenate strings in many programming languages, including JavaScript. In addition, it can be used as a unary operator to increase the size of a number by 1. For example: var number = 3; var result = number++;

This code creates a variable named number and assigns it the value 3. Then, it creates another variable named result that contains the value 4. This is because when you use the plus sign as a unary operator, it increases the size of whatever is on its left side by 1. So, in this case, we increased the number by 1 to get its new value (4).

In addition, the plus sign can be used as a binary operator to add two numbers together. For example: var sum = 1 + 2; This code creates a variable named sum that contains the value 3 because it adds 1 and 2 together (1 + 2).

Strings in C and C++

A string is a sequence of characters. In C and C++, they are represented as arrays of char.

String literals in C and C++ are sequences of characters surrounded by double quotes ("). For example:

```
"Hello" // Strings are zero-indexed
```

Note that strings are case-sensitive by default. For example, "Hello" != 'HELLO' or 'hello'. You can also make them case insensitive using the following syntax: "Hello."

Strings can be concatenated using the + operator: "I hate this" + " language."

Strings in C#

C# is a powerful, type-safe, object-oriented programming language that enables developers to build various applications for the .NET Framework and Mono. Microsoft developed it within its .NET initiative and later approved as a standard by ECMA (ECMA-334) and ISO (ISO/IEC 23270:2006). C# is one of several languages used with the .NET framework.

The Common Language Infrastructure (CLI) is the runtime environment for all CLI languages. The CLI provides support for binary machine code generation, platform independence, and security features, including native data protection, application domains, and garbage collection.

If You Master These Data Structures, You Can Solve Almost Any Problem

Because of this, it's worth learning about the different data structures and how they work. Data structures are important because they allow us to store information in a way that makes searching and sorting faster and more efficient. They're used in many different applications, such as databases and operating systems—you'll find them everywhere!

Chapter 4

Algorithms

An algorithm is a set of instructions for solving a problem. It is a step-by-step process that can be followed to reach the desired outcome.

What Is an Algorithm?

An algorithm is a set of instructions that tell the computer how to solve a problem. These instructions are written in a language the computer understands, and the computer can carry them out in any order.

As you might imagine, computers do not understand English or other natural languages often used when we describe problems to people. So instead of writing algorithms in these languages, we write them in codes that computers understand (often called programming languages).

Techniques of Algorithm Design

The techniques of algorithm design include heuristics, optimization, and the use of high-level languages. Heuristics are shortcuts that can be used to find good solutions to problems. Optimization is improving a solution by making it faster or more efficient. Using high-level languages such as Python or Java makes it easier for humans to write computer programs because they don't have to deal with the low-level details of how computers work. Debuggers are special programs that allow programmers to see what's happening inside their code as they write it; this lets them track down bugs by examining variable values and tracing execution paths through the program structure.

Characteristics of an Algorithm

You may be familiar with the term "algorithm," but what exactly is an algorithm?

An algorithm is a finite set of instructions used to solve a problem. In other words, it's a set of steps that can be applied repeatedly to produce the same result each time.

- **For all positive numbers x:** If $2x < y$ then $x < y + 1$

Properties of an Algorithm

When designing an algorithm, there are several properties that you may want to have:

- **Efficiency**: The time and space complexity of the algorithm. In other words, how long does it take to run? How much memory does it use?

- **Correctness**: Does the algorithm give correct results? Is it free from bugs? Can you find any examples where it will return incorrect results or even crash your program?

- **Clarity**: The algorithms should be as clear as possible. It should be easy for anyone who reads them (even non-programmers) to understand what they do and why they do so in this manner (i.e., don't write highly abstracted code). Try not to use tricks like macros or inline assembly; those are usually used when writing low-level code that only experts can understand because no one else knows how these things work internally!

Algorithms Are the Foundation of All Computer Programs

An algorithm is a set of rules for solving problems or making decisions.

For example, if you have a problem to solve, like "how many apples do I need to buy so that each apple has 2 pounds on it?" an algorithm would be:

1. Weigh each apple and add up the weights.

2. Multiply this total by two.

3. Subtract one apple from your result for every pound over two pounds per apple.

This is an example of an algorithm that could be used in a computer program (like FruitBasket2).

Recursion and Iteration

Recursion

Recursion is a programming technique that allows a function to call itself. The exact meaning of recursion varies from language to language, but in general:

- A recursive function calls itself (either directly or indirectly). This may happen for several reasons—to repeat an operation, solve problems that can be solved by dividing them into smaller and simpler problems, etc.

- Recursive functions are often used when iterative solutions do not work because they deal with infinities or very large numbers.

A few examples of recursive functions include factorial(), fibonacci(), and merge sort()

Iteration

Iteration is repeating a sequence of steps until some condition is met. The repetition is controlled by a loop, which typically has three parts:

- The initialization phase, where you initialize the loop's variables;

- The test phase, where you test whether the loop should continue (this may also be called termination); and

- The update phase is where you update any values that will affect future iterations of the loop.

Once a piece of code has been repeated "N" times (where "N" is determined during initialization), it will stop executing and move on to whatever comes next in your program.

Recursion and Iteration

Recursion and iteration are not the same. Recursion uses a function to call itself until it hits a base case, which stops calling. In contrast, iteration is the process of executing code multiple times in a row without using any sort of recursion.

Recursion and iteration are two ways of performing the same action repeatedly.

Search and Sort

Search and Sort is a Python library that provides two convenient methods to search and sort lists, dictionaries, and other sequences of objects. It's useful for finding things in lists and dictionaries— for example when you want to find all the times a word appears in a text document or where it appears most frequently. You can also use Search And Sort to sort list items from least to greatest or vice versa.

Search And Sort uses an algorithm called "Binary Search Tree" (BST), which is very efficient for sorting data sets with many elements but does not guarantee that it will always return results sorted correctly. e.g., if there is missing data).

Handy Hints

The sort() method sorts a list in place. To sort an entire list, pass it to the sort() method like this:

```Python
my_list = [1, 19, 20]

sort(my_list)
```

This will return a sorted copy of `my_list.` Passing None instead of `my_list` will cause Python to use the current value of the global environment as your list to sort (which means you can pass anything, and it'll be sorted). You can also pass in any other iterable object, such as a list or string that you want to use as your list argument.

Function

The def statement is the simplest way to define a function in Python.

If you want to call it later, you can use the name of your function as an expression anywhere that takes in a single argument and evaluates it.

You can also return multiple values from a function by using multiple return statements inside your function body. This is often useful when you need to return different types of data or objects (like strings) from different parts of your code. Of course, you may choose not to use return in some cases (e.g., if you are just using an expression to calculate what has been returned).

Lastly, you can raise errors inside functions by using the raise keyword followed by an exception name or type object after it's been defined in except clauses below. This will cause any program flow to be diverted into this block until something else catches that error using try except blocks elsewhere in your program. Otherwise, control will go back up through whatever called this specific call site (plus anything nested within it), continuing execution normally afterward until something else raises another error. Errors don't stop flowing until they're caught somewhere else - which means methods are often used for error handling since they tend not to be as deep in the call stack.

Diminutive Search

It's great to be able to search and sort data in Python, but how can we make our searches even more powerful?

We could use dictionaries, lists, sets, tuples, or strings as keys. However, sometimes it would be useful to have a way of searching through the contents of one variable or another. For example, if you wanted to search for "apple" in a string called fruit_list, you'd have no choice but to use regular expressions and hope for the best! This can lead to inefficient searches if your dictionary has many items.

The solution is a diminutive search (or "the tiny"), which uses objects specially designed for efficient searching. They're shorter than normal variables because they store only the values needed by a particular method rather than all its attributes at once, like other types do (like strings).

How to Sort an Array or List

To sort an array, use the sort() function.

- The first argument is a comparison function that determines how elements of the array are compared.

- The second argument is a value to be returned if the first argument returns true. If no return value is specified, undefined is used by default (which, in effect, causes nothing to happen).

Sorting a Dictionary By Keys in Python

If you have a dictionary of key-value pairs and want to sort it by the keys, you can use the sorted() function. To see how this works, start with an empty dictionary:

```
>>> d = {}
>>> d['a'] = 1
>>> d['b'] = 2
```

And now call sorted() on your dictionary:

```
>>> sorted(d) # Returns ['a', 'b']
```

If you want to sort a list by the values, use this code:

```
>>> sorted([1,2,3], key=lambda x: x) # Returns
[1, 2, 3]
```

If you have a dictionary of key-value pairs and want to sort it by the keys, you can use the sorted() function. To see how this works, start with an empty dictionary:

```
>>> d = {} >>> d['a'] = 1 >>> d['b'] = 2
```

And now call sorted() on your dictionary:

```
>>> sorted(d) # Returns ['a', 'b']
```

Sorting a Dictionary By Values in Python

To sort a dictionary by its values in Python, you can use the sorted() function. The syntax is:

```
sorted(dictionary, reverse=True)
```

If you set the reverse parameter to True, it will sort the items in ascending order (A-Z). If you set it to False, it will sort them in descending order (Z-A).

This is a very handy tool to have in your toolbox. It makes searching through large datasets much faster and more efficient. The ability to sort arrays by multiple properties at once is also very useful, especially if you're working with data from different people or teams who may not have used consistent conventions when entering data into their columns.

Backtracking in Algorithms

The most famous example of backtracking is the 8-puzzle. In this puzzle, there are 8 pieces, each numbered from 1 to 8. The goal is to put all of them in order by sliding them around (without rotating any number). This is easy if you have a computer—just set up some if-statements that check for collisions and move only when none exist—but it can be quite difficult for humans! It turns out that humans can solve this problem using something called backtracking: they try every possible combination until they find one that works.

What Is Backtracking?

Backtracking is an algorithm that tries to find the best possible solution to a problem. It's used in games like chess, for example, to determine whether a move is allowed and if it's possible to capture all of your opponent's pieces. The n-queens problem is another example where backtracking is useful: this famous puzzle involves placing n queens on an n x n board so they don't threaten each other (i.e., not attacking the same square).

Backtracking can also be used as part of algorithms that search through all possible solutions until they find one that meets their requirements or criteria. For example, consider this question: how many different ways can you put five books on a shelf? This can be answered easily by simply moving through all possibilities one at a time until you've tried each; however, there are over 1020 ways to do this! This means that no matter how powerful your computer might be—or how much time we allow for our algorithm—it will still take us forever, just considering every possibility before we begin finding answers we're happy with!

The n-Queens Problem

Backtracking is best demonstrated with the n-Queens problem. We need to place n chess queens on a n x n chessboard so that no two attack each other to address this difficulty. (If two queens are in the same row, column, or diagonal, they will fight each other.)

Examples

The n-queens problem is a classic example of a problem that requires backtracking. In this problem, you are given an array of n integers and must place n queens on the board so that no queen threatens any other. If you have never heard of the n-queens problem, I highly recommend looking it up! The solution is relatively simple, but the process involves many potential blind alleys.

A different example of backtracking is the knight's tour puzzle (also known as a knight's path). This puzzle involves placing all but one of a chess set's pieces on an 8x8 board so that each square has exactly one piece on it. There are no repeated moves from one move to another—the knight must visit every square exactly once and return to its starting position at some point during this journey. Here again, we see how backtracking allows us to explore many possible solutions before choosing which ones seem most promising based on certain criteria (in this case, whether or not there are repeated moves).

Backtracking Is Often Tricky and Difficult to Implement the Algorithm

Backtracking is a useful algorithm, but it can be tricky to implement. It's often used to solve problems with no solution, such as finding the shortest route through all the houses in a neighborhood. This problem has no obvious answer because there is not one perfect route through every house—a traveler can get trapped by two houses on one street that are too far apart for any other house between them (and thus must take an inconvenient detour). The same problem applies when deciding where to go for dinner: there's no way of knowing which restaurant will be best until after you've eaten at each one.

Some solutions are better than others. However: if you're deciding whether or not to eat at a restaurant based on its Yelp reviews, then reading all of those reviews would likely lead you toward a more informed decision. In this case, backtracking makes sense because we want our algorithm's first solution.

Dynamic Programming and Greedy Algorithms

Greedy algorithms and dynamic programming are two crucial concepts in algorithm design. They are often used together, focusing on solving problems by dividing them into smaller subproblems. The main difference is that a greedy algorithm always chooses the best possible solution at each step. In contrast, dynamic programming uses an optimal plan to solve multiple subproblems simultaneously.

Greedy Algorithms

Greedy algorithms are algorithms that make the best choice at each step. They are used when you don't know the whole problem or have limited time to solve a problem. The most straightforward greedy algorithm is "pick the first item from a list." This might seem like an odd choice for a greedy algorithm—why pick one item over all others? Because it's easy! It takes no time at all to do and can help you get started on solving more significant problems later.

The critical difference between dynamic programming and greedy algorithms is that dynamic programming allows for backtracking (changing your mind about your previous decision), while greediness does not allow this.

Dynamic Programming

Dynamic programming is a technique for solving problems by breaking them into subproblems of the same type. Dynamic programming uses recursion to solve issues and is often used to solve optimization problems.

The key difference between dynamic programming and other approaches is that it allows us to solve problems with overlapping and non-overlapping subproblems. In contrast, greedy algorithms only allow for non-overlapping subproblems, and backtracking algorithms only allow for overlapping subproblems.

Greedy Algorithms vs. Dynamic Programming

Greedy algorithms are better for small problems. Dynamic programming is a good way to solve many problems, but not all problems can be solved with dynamic programming.

Dynamic Programming can solve problems that are not greedy algorithms because it's more general than Greedy Algorithms.

Greedy algorithms and dynamic programming provide powerful tools for solving problems that have multiple solutions.

Bit Operations

Basic Bit Operations

Bitwise operations are performed on the individual bits of a binary number. For example, if you wanted to set the second bit from the left in your number, you would use this code:

```python
number = 10011011

bit_count = number & 0b00011100
```

This would set bit 2 to 1 (1 + 4) while leaving all other bits unchanged. This can be useful if you want to operate on just one piece of data without affecting any other part. If we wanted to check if our number was even or odd by performing a comparison between its number of 1s and 0s, we could do so using this code:

```python
import math

if (((number & 0b11111110) == 0b01100000)) {

print("It's even!")

} else {

print("It's odd!")

}
```

This would print out "It's odd!" because the number has more 1s than 0s.

Operation &

- AND operation is used to compare two bits.

- AND operations are used to set bits to 0.

- AND operations are used to clear bits to 0.

- AND operations are used to combine two-bit patterns into a single-bit pattern.

Operation |

BITWISE OR OPERATION

The bitwise OR operation is a binary operation that performs a bit-by-bit logical inversion on each pair of corresponding bits of two binary integers and produces the result as a single integer.

Operation ^

The bitwise XOR operator is denoted with the caret symbol (^). The result of a bitwise XOR operation is 1 if the bits are different and 0 if they are equal. For example, let's say you want to perform a logical operation on two numbers:

```
  __|__ | __|__

  1101 ^ 1010 => 1110 (1 ^ 1 = 1)

  1010 ^ 1101 => 0100 (0 ^ 0 = 0)
```

The result of the bitwise XOR operation is a 1 in the first-bit position where there is a difference between the two operands and 0 everywhere else.

The result of the bitwise XOR operation is a 1 in the first-bit position where there is a difference between the two operands and 0 everywhere else. For example, let's say you want to perform a logical operation on two numbers:

```
  1101 ^ 1010 => 1110 (1 ^ 1 = 1) 1010 ^ 1101 =>
  0100 (0 ^ 0 = 0)
```

Operation <<

The left shift operator shifts the binary representation of a number to the left. Let's look at some examples.

In binary, 1101100 represents 5 in decimal. If we apply a left shift operator, we get 1001110 which is 16 in decimal. You can see that bit 3 has been moved over by 1 place, and bit 2 has been dropped off because it was shifted out of existence!

The result above is equivalent to multiplying 5 by 4: 5 * 4 = 20 / 2 = 10 (the number on the right). Since this is not very useful, let's try another example with similar numbers: 1101100 / 1001110 = 1 (because 1101100 divides evenly into 1001110). This means that you can use division and addition/subtraction with <<!

Operation >>

The shift operator, >>, shifts the bits in a value to the right. The leftmost bit is shifted in, and the rightmost bit is shifted out. The new value is always a nonnegative integer. So if you have an integer variable x and you want to shift it one place to the right, your code would look like this:

```
>> x = 1<<1;
```

In this example, x would equal 2.

The right shift operator is a bit more complicated. It shifts all bits in a value to the right, discarding any bits that are shifted out. The only requirement is that the new value must be an integer. So if you have an integer variable x and you want to shift it one place to the right, your code would look like this: >> x = 1>>>1; In this example, x would equal 4.

Chapter 5

Code with High Quality

There are many reasons developers should strive to write high-quality code.

If a Bug Is Introduced into a High-Quality Code Base, the Bug Can More Easily Be Found and Fixed

First, if a bug is introduced into a high-quality code base, the bug can more easily be found and fixed. The code is testable, so it's easy to write tests for new features that ensure they don't break existing functionality. And because the codebase is well-structured and maintainable, fixing bugs also becomes easier.

Finally, because the code is readable (and thus easy for programmers to understand), there are fewer bugs in the first place! On top of all, these benefits stem from building and maintaining good developer relationships: developers who feel appreciated will be more productive.

Code Is More Testable If It Has Fewer Dependencies, Is Cohesive, and Is Loosely Coupled

- Code with fewer dependencies is more testable. If you have a class that depends on another class, you'll need to create an instance of the second one to test that first class. This can be time-consuming and expensive if the second class has many dependencies—or worse yet if those dependencies themselves have dependencies!

- Isolated classes with single responsibilities are easier to test than classes with multiple responsibilities.

- Code with high cohesion is easier to test because it's simpler for developers who don't know about its internals or "how everything fits together."

- Dependency injection (DI) frameworks like Dagger allow developers to write code against interfaces rather than concrete implementations. This makes it much easier for testing since there's no need to mock concrete versions during tests; just inject your interface into your codebase!

High-Quality Code Evolves More Easily Because It Is Easier to Change

The best way to ensure that your code will evolve easily is to write high-quality code in the first place. High-quality code is easier to change, test, and maintain.

If you write high-quality code, it will be easier to change because it has a small surface area and follows a consistent pattern. It's also easier to test because you have more confidence that the tests will work. A well-written piece of software often has fewer bugs than low-quality ones, so there's less time spent dealing with bugs (and fixing them). If something does go wrong, less time is spent on maintenance.

High-Quality Code Is Easier to Read and Understand

High-quality code is easier to read, understand, debug, maintain and extend.

- **Readability**: You can easily read a high-quality piece of code because it follows established rules of good coding practices. It has a consistent structure and uses meaningful variable names and comments where appropriate. The author has avoided writing long lines of code or complicated constructs that you would need to spend hours trying to understand.

- **Understandability**: This allows you as the reader (or future developer) to understand what each part of the program does without having to dive into its implementation details or reverse engineer it by looking at other parts of the same program or its libraries (which may not be available). It also helps you debug because if something goes wrong with a particular line, there are only a few places that could cause problems instead of thousands. For example, in case such a situation happens on a large project where all developers work together without following standards!

Entire Systems Comprised of Low-Quality Code Can Cost 10 Times as Much to Maintain as High-Quality Systems

You may think that you're not spending a lot of time trying to fix bugs in your code, but the cost of maintaining low-quality software can be substantial.

The average cost for fixing a bug is between $5,000 and $10,000 (depending on the industry). This is extremely expensive compared to other costs in your business, like marketing or profits – especially if you have thousands of bugs that need fixing!

Software Should Be Easy to Use By Users

- Easy to use

- Easy to understand

- Easy to learn

- Easy to change

- Easy to administer

- Easy to extend (grow, evolve)

- Easy to integrate with other software

There Are Many Reasons Developers Should Strive to Write High-Quality Code

- The code does what it's supposed to do.

- The code is easy to change as requirements evolve, or even just as the developer's mind changes about how best to implement something; this is called "elegance of expression" and is impossible if your code is badly structured and hard to understand!

- The structure of your program matches the structure of its problem domain (i.e., an object-oriented design). It makes it easy for other programmers (including yourself) to understand what's happening inside that domain through automated tests written in plain English. And therefore avoids having bugs later on down the line due to only partially understood behavior from earlier iterations where no one could tell exactly what was going wrong when things went wrong!

Simplify Your Solutions

- Simplification

- Understandability

- Maintainability

- Debug-ability

- Testability

- Extendibility (the ability to extend the functionality)

- Reusability (the ability to reuse code)

Are you concerned that this will make your code less readable? Don't be. The idea is not to sacrifice clarity for simplicity but to find a balance between them. In other words, we're after an approach that maximizes both readability and simplicity.

Writing Clean, High-Quality Code Is Important to Creating Good Software

Writing clean, high-quality code is important to creating good software. High-quality code can be easier to understand and maintain, easier to test, easier to extend, refactor and parallelize.

The layout of the page (or, in this case, a document) can help you make sense of things on the page quickly by breaking it up into chunks that you can easily digest. A good layout also helps separate content from presentation (CSS). This separation makes it easy for other people working on your project or your team to add/change/remove content without changing how it looks on the front end.

The Code Does What It's Supposed to Do

The code does what it's supposed to do. The code does what it says it does.

The code does not do what it's not supposed to do, and the code does not do what it says it doesn't do.

The Code Is Easy to Change as Requirements Evolve

A program that is easy to change will make your life easier when requirements evolve. Here are some things you can do:

- Minimize coupling between components of your application by keeping them independent, distinct, and loosely coupled. This makes it easier to reuse code in different contexts (for example, an HTML page with a dropdown menu can be used on any other web page). It also makes it easier to replace one component with another if necessary -- say, if there's a bug or security vulnerability in one component but not the others.

- Ensure that each piece of code has only a few dependencies on other classes/methods/etc. so that individual pieces can be easily modified without affecting other parts of the system too much. Doing this means building abstractions (abstract classes) at appropriate levels within an application's hierarchy; this help defines boundaries between high-level functionality and low-level implementation details such as data storage mechanisms.

The Code Is Well-Structured

When you write code, you want it to be easy for other developers to understand and modify. Therefore, good code should be well-structured.

A piece of well-structured code is organized to make it easy to understand and maintain. Well-structured code supports the problem domain by using appropriate data structures, and it also supports the language using idiomatic language constructs. We'll look at each of these in more detail below:

- Organizing your code according to its purpose or problem domain can make it easier for others to read your code because they have a context for understanding what the various parts are doing, which makes it much faster than reading disjointed chunks of code without any obvious point of reference. The same principle applies no matter what programming language you're using: If someone has never seen this specific syntax before, adding comments explaining how a particular block works can help them get up-to-speed much faster than if there were no explanation at all.

The Code Is Efficient but Not Needlessly So

You should aim to write as efficient code as possible, but not more. In other words, the code you produce should be as efficient as necessary and no less so.

If your program has many optimization opportunities, it's okay if your code is initially inefficient. You can always optimize later when you have time to look into it. But if your program doesn't have many optimization opportunities—or even zero opportunities—then making an effort to make your code more efficient may not be worth it.

There Are Lots of Automated Tests That Prove the Code Works

Tests are an essential part of any good development process. They allow you to verify that your code does what it's supposed to and can be used by other developers as a reference for future changes.

But tests aren't just about proving that the code works; they should be written by the developers, not users or customers. And they should be automated, so they frequently run with minimal human intervention. Finally, tests shouldn't just check for errors but also ensure that the program works as expected under various conditions (such as when there isn't enough memory available).

Finally, test-driven development encourages writing small pieces of functionality before adding more complex features later on—this helps prevent bugs from occurring earlier in development cycles than necessary.

Fixing One Bug Doesn't Seem to Introduce Others

The best way to prevent new bugs from being introduced when you fix a bug is to write code that's easy to understand and easy to change. A big part is having good variable names, which can help you figure out what the code does so you can make changes.

However, this also means that fixing one thing tends not to introduce other problems. When writing code and seeing a problem, there is often more than one thing wrong with it (maybe even several things). Fixing just one of those things might make it easier for us or someone else in the future to find more problems with our code.

Creating high-quality code is not only important for your business, but it's also essential to the success of your entire team. Good code will make it easier to manage changes in the future, save time and money now, avoid bugs in the production and testing phases of development workflows, and reduce maintenance costs over time.

By following these tips, you can create more robust applications that are easier to maintain over time without sacrificing the initial implementation cost or time needed for development.

Strategies to Handle Errors

As a developer, one of the most common and frustrating errors is getting errors in code. Here are some tips to help you deal with them:

Use the Debugging Tools

Next, use the debugging tools in your IDE.

If you don't have an IDE, try using the debugger with your language.

If you don't have a debugger and there's no debugger available for your language (or if you're using an older version of that language), try using the browser's developer tools.

Try to Isolate the Problem (This May Help You Find the Cause of the Problem)

So, you've got an error that you can't seem to fix. What do you do?

Well, the first thing is to try and isolate the problem. Next, you want to narrow down what is causing your error so that it's easier for someone else (or even yourself) to fix it. This may sound like a simple task, but most of the time, this can be very difficult, depending on how complex your code base is.

Here are some examples:

- Suppose you're working with JavaScript and have an issue with a specific browser or device. In that case, it might be more straightforward because all we need is one browser/device combination, and then we can swap out its code for another one that works properly (such as Chrome Beta instead of regular Chrome). However, if we worked with CSS instead, things would get much more difficult since there are so many different browsers. Each supports different CSS features, so identifying which exact browser-specific bug caused our issue could prove challenging even for someone experienced working across multiple browsers and devices!

- Another example would be SQL queries where it's easy to look at whether something went wrong while running them - e.g., maybe there was just one small typo somewhere that caused everything else to fail after that point to fail too? Or maybe there's some other reason why those queries failed? These issues are relatively easy because they're usually pretty straightforward (and often caused by human error). But imagine if, instead, we had thousands upon thousands of lines of code containing hundreds upon hundreds of variables used across multiple files. This could take hours or days to figure out where exactly something went wrong!"

Research Your Error Message to See Example Fixes

As you learn more about the language, errors will become less frequent. However, you might still encounter bugs while working on projects or in class. If this happens, try to research your error message to see example fixes. For example, if you run into an error that says, "The compiler encountered a problem with the code and could not continue," then check online for other people's solutions for this issue (searching "error compiler cannot continue" might be helpful). If you can't find anything useful online, ask someone else for help by posting on StackOverflow or asking your instructor or TA directly!

Communicate with Others about the Problem, Especially More Experienced Coders

If you've never done this before and need help, don't hesitate to ask for it. Don't let the fear of looking stupid prevent you from reaching out—it's much better than spending hours trying to figure out a problem someone else could solve in minutes.

If there aren't any resources available (like forums or Stack Overflow), create one yourself! Then, if enough people use your resource, it can turn into an invaluable resource for others.

Take a Break If You're Frustrated, and Try Again Later

If you're experiencing code errors, take a break if you are frustrated. You may have failed to fix the error and give up, but often there is no need to be upset or discouraged. Instead of trying again immediately, give yourself some time to cool off and come back later with fresh eyes. For example, if you are in the middle of fixing an error that has been plaguing you for days or weeks, try taking a walk outside for 10 minutes. This can help refresh your mind and allow you to see things from a different perspective which could lead to new ideas on how to solve the problem.

Another way to help is by getting some fresh air by heading outdoors for about 30 minutes (we all need breaks now and then). This will also provide mental space away from electronics, so it helps de-stress our brains after working hard on something difficult like programming issues!

In addition: don't try fixing error codes when tired. This creates more problems than solutions because our brain cannot function properly when exhausted due to a lack of sleep or restful activities where we don't think much (e.g., watching movies).

Read Through Your Code and Make Sure It Matches What You Want to Do

- Read through your code and make sure it matches what you want to do.

- Check that you used the right syntax. For example, if you were trying to construct a query with two tables but accidentally inserted an extra "and" between them, this could cause an error when executing the query.

- Check that you used the right data types for each variable and column.

- Check that all functions were called correctly, including any optional arguments specified by their documentation (if applicable).

- Make sure that your code is consistent with other parts of your program and with "common sense," or else errors may arise when running large-scale programs.

Read Your Code Aloud to Get Another Perspective on It

Reading your code aloud is a great way to find errors in your writing. You can also have another person read it aloud to you or use a text-to-speech tool like Google Translate or Microsoft Speech Platform. This can be especially helpful if you're unfamiliar with the language used in the code (for example, if you're using English but not familiar enough with Python).

In addition to reading out loud, ask someone else who knows nothing about coding and has no idea what's going on to read over your writing. They may be able to spot errors you couldn't because their programming knowledge isn't ingrained into their brain yet!

It's Never Fun When You Get an Error Message, But There Are Ways to Handle Them Well and Move Forward

You can't always fix the error, but you can learn from it. The first thing to do is read the error message carefully. What does it tell you? Did it give any information on what went wrong?

Try to figure out what caused the problem and see if there's a way around it in future projects. For example, if your code has been giving errors because of missing references or dependencies, maybe you need to change your programming style so that things are clearer and easier to manage.

If there was an unexpected error message when running a program (as opposed to one from compiling), ask someone who knows more about this stuff than yourself how they would fix it - perhaps even check out some tutorials together! You'll learn something new about code writing and gain valuable experience for future jobs/projects."

There's no way to get around errors. The best thing you can do is take them in stride and handle them calmly. If you're getting frustrated, take a break and return later; this will make your code clearer and easier to read. And if all else fails, remember that there are people who want to help—even if they're not always available at first glance!

Chapter 6

Approaches to Visualizing Problems and Their Solutions

There are several approaches to solutions in coding, and they all have their own pros and cons.

Mirror of Binary Trees

A mirror of Binary Trees is a data structure that stores all the nodes in a binary tree along with its mirror image. The mirror image of each node is stored at the predefined place after every right-leaf node.

Problem

In this section, we'll cover the process of visualizing a problem by mirroring binary trees. The problem will be to find all solutions for the following equations:

- $7x + 11y = 77$

- $2x - y = 1$

We'll write the syntax in an understandable way for each equation and then use that syntax to create an algorithm. Then we'll visualize it by mirroring binary trees. The first step is writing down the syntax of how you want to see your answer (the thing you will be looking for). For example:

```c++\r

7x +11y = 77\r

\r 2x-y = 1\r ```

The second step is to write down the syntax of how you want to find your answer. This is called an algorithm. For example:

```c++\r int x = 7; int y = 11; int z = 77; \r

while (z >= 0) {//loop until we reach zero! if (x + y == z) {//if the sum of x and y equals z, then break out of the loop printf("%d", x + y); } else {//otherwise keep going through each possible solution for x and y until one works! } } ```

### *Mirror of Binary Trees*

The mirror of a binary tree is another binary tree where all the nodes in the left subtree are duplicated on the right and vice versa. This means that each node in one sub-tree is paired with its mirroring node in another sub-tree, like so:

Tree 1 Tree 2

- (1) / \ / \ / \

- 2 3 4 5 6 7 8 9 * (1)

As you can see, trees 1 and 2 have the same structure: binary trees with the root node at the top, the left child at bottom level 0, the right child at level 1, etc. The only difference between these two trees is that tree 1 has all its nodes duplicated on tree 2. i.e., if we wanted to write down an array containing every single value stored inside tree 1 (and this applies to any kind of data structure). Then we'd just need half as many elements as we would need if we were writing down only half of its values (i.e., we'd need twice more elements).

### Solution - Recursive Approach

You can use the recursive approach to solve this problem. Here is the code for it:

- **Recursive function:**

```c++

void mirror(BinaryTree *root) {

if (root->left != nullptr) { // If left child
exists...
```

- **Mirroring recursive call:**

```c++

```c++ if (root->left->right != nullptr) { // If
right child exists... mirror(root->left); } else
{ // Otherwise, only in case of empty binary
tree return; } ```
```

This will call itself recursively until it finds a leaf node or reaches the root.
```

```c++

if (root->left != nullptr)

{ // If left child exists... mirror(root-
>left); } else { // Otherwise, only in case of
empty binary tree return; }
```

Algorithm

The algorithm is fairly straightforward. First, we will traverse the tree in both directions and record the nodes where the binary trees are equal. In this way, we can construct a new binary tree that represents only those elements that are common to both trees.

Let's start with an example:

Given the following two binary trees:

```
Tree 1: 1 / \ 2 3 / \ 4 5 6
```

```
Tree 2: 7 / \ 8 9 10 11 12 13 14 15 16 17 18 19
20 21 22 23 24 25 26 27 28 29 30 31 32 33 34 35
36 37 38 39 40 41 42 43 44 45 46 47 48 49 50 51
52 53 54 55 56 57 58 59 60 61 62 63 64 65 66 67
68 69 70 71 72 73 74 75 76 77 78 79 80 81 82 83
84 85 86 87 88 89 90 91 92 93 94 95 96 97
```

We want to find out if they share any common elements. Here is the algorithm:

1. Start with the first tree (Tree 1) 2. Traverse the nodes in depth-first order, creating another binary tree (Tree 3).

2. Compare the two binary trees: 4. If you find an equal node in both binary trees, then you can mark this node with a unique identifier (say, id).

3. If you don't find a common node, go to the next tree and repeat steps 2-4 until all trees have been traversed (or there are no more common elements). 6. Once all the trees have been visited, return a new binary tree that contains only those nodes with an id associated with them.

This process is called a "common prefix" or "prefix-sum" of the trees. The output of this algorithm is a tree where each node has an integer associated with it, representing the number of common nodes between all trees. Let's take a look at some example output:

```
Output 1: 1 0 4 2 0 3 0 2 1 4 1 2 3 5 6 8 7 9 10
11 12 13 14 15 16 17 18 19 20 21 22 23 24 25 26
27 28 29 30 31 32 33 34 35 36 37 38 39 40 41 42
43 44 45 46 47 48 49 50 51 52 53 54 55 56 57 58
59 60 61 62 63 64 65 66 67 68 69 70 71 72 73

Output 2: 1 0 4 2 0 3 0 2 1 4 1 2 3 5 6 8 7 9 10
11 12 13 14 15 16 17 18 19 20 21 22 23 24 25 26
27 28 29 30 31 32 33 34 35 36 37 38 39 40 41 42
43 44 45 46 47 48 49 50 51 52 53 54 55 56 57 58
59 60 61 62 63 64 65 66 67 68 69 70 71 72 73 74
75 76 77 78 79 80 81 82 83 84 85 86 87 88 89 90
91 92 93 94 95 96 97 98 99 100 101 102 103 104
105 106 107 108 109 110 111 112 113 114 115 116
117 118 119 120 121 122 123 124 125 126 127 128
129 130 131 132 133 134 135

Output 3: 1 0 4 2 0 3 0 2 1 4 1 2 3 5 6 8 7 9 10
11 12 13 14 15 16 17 18 19 20 21 22 23 24 25 26
27 28 29 30 31 32 33 34 35 36 37 38 39 40 41 42
```

```
43 44 45 46 47 48 49 50 51 52 53 54 55 56 57 58
59 60 61 62 63 64 65 66 67 68 69 70 71 72 73 74
75 76 77 78 79 80 81 82 83 84 85 86 87 88 89 90
91 92 93 94 95 96 97 98 99 100 101 102 103 104
105 106 107 108 109 110 111 112 113 114 115 116
117 118 119 120 121 122 123 124 125 126 127 128
129 130 131 132 133 134
```

Clone Complex Lists

When data gets complex, it's important to find a way of solving it. Lists are one of the most common structures in computer science, and they can get pretty big. Unfortunately, while they're useful, they don't always scale well as their data increases in size. There are ways around this problem, though! It turns out that lists can be cloned with an algorithm called "memoization."

What Are Complex Lists?

Complex lists are a very common data structure in coding. They are lists of other lists, which can be nested to any depth. For example:

```java
List> complex = new ArrayList>();

complex.add(new ArrayList(Arrays.asList("a")));

complex.add(new ArrayList(Arrays.asList("b"))));
```

and so on! Each outer list is an arraylist of strings, with each inner one being another arraylist of strings.

Complex Lists Can Be Cloned with the Right Algorithm

As a developer, you've probably had the experience of trying to clone a complex list. You know, those long lists with different types of data and some logic attached to them? To make matters worse, your boss has just asked you to add more items together from two different complex lists.

Well, as it turns out, there is an algorithm that can help you do this! The key is understanding how the algorithm works for each type of data in your list:

Complex Lists

The structure of the complex list must be understood by the cloning algorithm (for example: "this complex list contains only images" or "this complex list contains text boxes").

The contents of this type of data must also be analyzed and understood (for example: "there are 10 image objects" or "there are 110 text box objects").

Simple Lists

The structure of the simple list must be understood by the cloning algorithm (for example: "This is a list of strings" or "this is a list of numbers"). The contents of this type of data must also be analyzed and understood (for example: "there are 10 string objects" or "there are 110 number objects").

Now that you know what to expect in your list let's talk about how the algorithm works. As you can see from the above descriptions, there are two main steps:

1. Analyze and understand the structure and contents of each type of data in your list, and

2. Cloning. The first step is performed by a specialized algorithm that I call a "list parser." This parser will analyze your lists (both complex and simple), extracting relevant information such as their structure and contents.

After this analysis has occurred, our algorithm will then take these data structures and use them to clone each item in your list.

Complex Lists: The first step is to parse each complex list. Once this has been done, we can analyze the structure of our data and know what type of object it is. For example: if we have a dictionary, we know it's a collection of key-value pairs. If we have an array, we know it's an ordered collection of values.

If we have a file, we know it's a collection of lines. If we have a list with complex items (i.e., objects), then we know that it's an ordered collection of objects. This is important because each type of object has its own set of rules for how to clone itself. For example, dictionaries can be cloned by making copies of their key-value pairs. Arrays can be cloned by creating new instances with the same values. Files can be cloned by copying all their contents into another file, and lists with complex items can be cloned by making copies of each item in the list.

Once we know what kind of object the list is, we can clone it by recursively calling ourselves on each item in the list. For example: if we have a list of dictionaries, we will call ourselves on each key-value pair; if we have a list of files, then we will call ourselves on each line; and so on.

As a concrete example, let's say we have a list of dictionaries (i.e., key-value pairs). We can clone this list by recursively calling ourselves on each key-value pair in the list:

```
list_of_dicts = [{'hi': 'there'}, {'bye':
'world'}]

cloned_list = [self.clone() for item in
list_of_dicts]
```

This will create a new list with the same key-value pairs as the original.

This clone solution is useful for cloning complex lists and can also be used in other types of problems that involve finding a solution to the same problem. For example, if we wanted to find all possible combinations of two numbers that sum up to 10, then we could also use this method! This is just one example among many uses for this algorithm--and hopefully, it will inspire you with new ideas.

Stack with Min Function

The stack is a simple data structure with two operations: push and pop. A stack can be implemented using an array, linked list, or queue. The first two cases are efficient for some algorithms but not all of them. The third one has O(1) time complexity in both cases (push and pop).

Problem

You have a stack, and you want to know the minimum value of its elements. This can be done constantly using the min function, but unfortunately, this function is not available in all programming languages. So how do you write your own?

Brute Force Solution

You can use brute force to find the minimum value in a stack.

First, define a function to return the minimum value of a stack:

def min(stack):

- Use a stack to store the values.

- Use pop() to remove the top value from the stack.

- Use min() to find the minimum value in your new, smaller stack.

Return the found minimum value. Next, use a stack to store the values. Use pop() to remove the top value from the stack. Use min() to find the minimum value in your new, smaller stack. Return the found minimum value.

For example, you could use the following code to find the minimum value in a stack: def min(stack): Use a stack to store the values. Use pop() to remove the top value from the stack. Use min()

to find the minimum value in your new, smaller stack. Return the found minimum value.

Optimized Solution

You can create an optimized solution by using a queue to store the elements of the stack. The most common data structure for this type of problem is a stack.

To optimize this further, however, we need something that can quickly search through our list of numbers and find their minimum value (or smallest element). This is where the min() function in Python comes into play!

You may already know how sorting algorithms work if you are familiar with other programming languages, such as Java or C++. In those languages, they have built-in functions like sort(), where they will compare each number against each other until they have found their correct place within the list based on some criteria (the biggest number goes first).

How to Write a Function to Retrieve the Minimum Value of a Stack in Constant Time

The first step is to write a function that takes an array of integers and returns the minimum value. It should run in constant time, which means it will take the same amount of time regardless of how many elements there are in the array. This particular function only works for arrays with no duplicate values. If you have a duplicate value in your input array, this function will return that value instead of your desired minimum.

The second step is to write code that tests whether or not our new min() function works correctly by simulating it several times with different inputs:

```python
import random

def main():

for _ in range(5):

arr = random.sample(range(20), 3) print("min:",
min(arr)) main() ```
```

This will generate five different arrays of integers and print out the minimum value. The output should look like this:

```
``` min: 4

min: 1

min: 2 min: 5

min: 2 ```
```

This shows that our function is working correctly. It returns the correct minimum value every time. The third step is to make the function more efficient by making it run in O(1) time rather than O(n2). This means that, for any given input size n, our function will take no more than 1 step (or operation) to run.

Push and Pop Sequence of Stacks

This code is based on correspondence between push and pop sequences of stacks.
```

The push and pop operations can be done in any order. Therefore, the push and pop operations sequence is called a Push-Pop sequence of stacks. As shown below, there are two possible stack configurations: one in which the top element is popped first (LIFO) and another in which it is pushed first (FIFO). The LIFO configuration means that elements are removed from bottom to top, while FIFO means that elements are inserted from top to bottom.

There Are Two Sequences Given, One Is the Push Sequence, and the Other Is a Pop Sequence

Push Sequence: 1, 2, 3, 4, 5 ... Pop Sequence: 1, 2, 5 ...

The Task Is to Find If the Given Order of Operations of Push and Pop on the Stack Can Be Possible or Not

The first step to achieving your goal is to set a deadline. You may want to think about how much time you want to put into training and how much you would like to dedicate every week. For example, if you want to lose weight but don't have much free time on your hands during the weekdays or weekends, you could try setting a goal of losing two pounds each week. This will prevent you from getting overwhelmed by trying to lose ten pounds in one month!

It is also important not just to come up with easy goals for yourself (like losing one pound per month). The key component here is setting goals that are challenging enough so that it takes some effort for you to accomplish them! It's important because otherwise, we become complacent after achieving our initial task, and things stop moving towards our ultimate goal.

Solution

The idea is to use a stack for the push sequence. For each i-th element in the pop sequence, if it's the same as the i-th element in the push sequence, then continue. Otherwise, start popping from the stack till we find the same element.

At last, if more elements are left in both pop and push sequences, then just return false.

The Sequence Then Continues. Otherwise, Start Popping from the Stack Till We Find the Same Element. Then, Finally, Check If the Stack Is Empty or Not

Now it's time to check if the stack is empty or not. If it is empty, then we are done. Otherwise, we need to continue popping from the stack till we find the same element in the next level. Finally, check if the stack is empty or not. If it is, we can say that no duplicate was found and return true or false.

If It Is Empty, Then the Order of Operation Can Be Possible; Otherwise, Not Possible

We can apply push and pop operations if the stack is empty. The empty condition is checked from the stack pointer; if it's false, we don't have to apply any push or pop operation on that stack.

Otherwise, if a stack is not empty, then we don't apply the order of operation for that particular stack.

The Algorithm of This Code Is Based on Correspondence between Push and Pop Sequences

The algorithm of this code is based on correspondence between push and pop sequences. Correspondence refers to the ability of two sets of data to be matched or paired up with each other.

In this case, we have a sequence of operations that pushes one element at a time onto the stack, then pops it off again in reverse order. The correspondence between these two operations can be used to check if the order of operations will lead to a valid stack or not:

- If you push an element onto your stack, then push another one on top of it, you know that when you want to pop them both off later (in reverse order), there will be nothing left after popping off both elements; therefore, this is an invalid sequence!

The same principle can be applied to any other valid push-pop sequence, including those that simultaneously push and pop multiple elements. For example:

You know that if you push two elements onto a stack, then pop them both off again in reverse order, there will be nothing left after popping off both elements; therefore, this is an invalid sequence!

We can see that the algorithm of this code is based on correspondence between push and pop sequences. The idea is to use a stack for the push sequence. For each i-th element in the pop sequence, if it's the same as an i-th element in the push sequence, then continue. Otherwise, start popping from the stack till we find the same element. Finally, check if the stack is empty or not. If it is empty, then the order of operation can be possible; otherwise not possible.

Chapter 7

Optimization

If you have ever written a computer program, you know that it can be a challenging task. However, once your code is written, you must then turn your attention to optimizing it. Optimization refers to the process of making your program run faster and use fewer resources while still performing its intended functions. "code optimization" refers to any technique or method used to improve performance by making changes to source code or its compilation process.

What Is Coding Optimization?

Coding optimization makes a program run faster and more efficiently by improving its source code.

This can be done using various techniques, such as microarchitectural optimizations (including instruction scheduling and memory access), program analysis to determine what parts of the code can be optimized, or even just good old-fashioned trial-and-error. Many modern compilers have built-in optimizers that take care of these tasks automatically; however, manual coding optimization is possible and often preferable when you need fine control over the production process.

Why Should We Care about Coding Optimization?

You have probably heard the term "coding optimization" before, but what does it mean? Coding optimization is the process of improving the efficiency of your code. In other words, ensuring your program runs as fast and efficiently as possible. The important thing to understand here is that this process can be done on any piece of code; if you're working with a piece of software or hardware in any way, you can always optimize it. However, there are times when we decide not to optimize our code because doing so would take too much time and effort.

Performance of a Program

- Compiled code is faster than interpreted code. Compiling code is faster than interpreted code because when you compile a program, the compiler creates an executable and stores it on the disk. When you run this executable, your computer can read the file from disk rather than having to interpret what was written in high-level language each time it runs.

- Code written in a high-level language is faster than code written in assembly language. This means that writing your program in C++ instead of directly in assembly language will make it run faster. There are no extra steps for your computer to go through before running your compiled executable, saving time overall.

- Code optimized for a specific CPU (central processing unit) will run more efficiently on that type of CPU than unoptimized code running on different CPUs due to differences between their internal architectures or instruction sets.*

Compiler Optimizations

In a nutshell, compiler optimizations result from a compiler's attempt to improve the performance of a program. Compilers can perform many different types of optimizations; some are more common than others, and some are more effective than others.

The first kind is code optimization. This means that if you write code similar to something else in your program (but perhaps not identical), it will likely result in a smaller file size or better execution time. For example, suppose you were writing a loop that prints out numbers 1 through 100 with print("%d," x) at each iteration:

```
for i in range(1, 101):

print("%d" % i)#
```

Programming Optimizations

When optimizing code, it's important to understand that there are some cases where you don't necessarily need to optimize. For example, if your program is working properly and running at a reasonable speed, you can leave it alone. You should also be aware that optimization can be extremely time-consuming and difficult to do manually. Some people consider this method of programming optimization a waste of time because the compiler will usually do it for you anyway—but we'll get into that later!

So what exactly does "programming optimization" mean? Simply put, make changes to your code to run more efficiently (and therefore faster). Of course, this isn't always necessary; if your program is working properly and running reasonably, then there may be no reason to change its source code! However, if there are ways in which performance could be improved without affecting functionality or usability - then why not take advantage of them?

Intersection of Sorted Arrays

This can be done in O(m+n) time and O(m+n) space when elements are distinct. When elements are not distinct, it can be done in O(m+n) time and O(m) space by iterating through the lists until a match is found, then moving on to the next one or eliminating repeats from a list.

The Intersection of Two Sorted Arrays

The intersection of two sorted arrays is a new sorted array that contains only elements common to both the input arrays. When elements are distinct, the intersection of two sorted arrays can be computed in O(m+n) time and O(m+n) space.

If the elements are distinct, we can use an efficient mergesort algorithm to compute their intersection.

Approach 1: O(M+N) Time and O(M+N) Space When Elements Are Distinct

- First, you can use a simple binary search to find the first element in the first list that is greater than or equal to the first element in the second list. You'll need to know how many elements are in each of your sorted arrays to know where to start your search.

- Then, do another binary search (by making corresponding changes) on each successive pair of lists until you've checked all pairs and found:

- The last element in one array is less than or equal to another array's last element; or * The first element in one array that is greater than another array's first element.

Approach 2: O(M+N) Time and O(M) Space When Elements Are Not Distinct

In this approach, we will use a hash table to store the intersections of sorted arrays. The idea is that given two lists, we can convert their elements into integers and then use them as indexes into a hash table that stores the intersections between them.

To see how this works, consider an example where we have three lists: [1], [2], and [3]. We want to find all of the intersections between these lists. To do so, we first need to convert each element in our first list into an integer (we'll use modulus division for now). So if our input list is [1], then its first element becomes 1:

```
1 = 1 mod 3 = 0
```

If our input list were actually [4] instead of just 1, then since 4 !=
2^k for some k, it would not map out properly using modulus
division. In other words:

```
4 = 4^k . Since k=0 does not work here

( 4 != 2^0 = 1 ),
```

we need a different approach.

Instead of modulus division, we will use the following algorithm: -
Choose a random integer k between 0 and the number of elements
in the input set. -Convert each element in our first list into an
integer (we'll use this new function called intval that converts
strings into integers) and then multiply it by k.

Combine the new integers into a single list. For example, if our first
input were [1], then this would give us:

```
[[0],[1]] = 1*k  [[2],[3],[4]] = 2*k + 3*k + 4^k
```

**Iterate Through the Lists Until a Match Is Found, Then Move
to the Next One or Eliminate Repeats in an Array**

To iterate through the lists until you find a match, do something
like this:

for i in range(len(list1)): # first loop to iterate through list1

if list2[i] == 3: # second check to determine if 3 is in your
array. If it is, then break out of the loop.

This means you've found a match!

Break: # I want to stop looping after locating this value (the last one).

else: # what happens if we don't find it? Try again and keep looking for a match!

The intersection of two sorted arrays is a problem that has been studied extensively. There are many different ways to do it, but often it comes down to whether the elements are distinct or not. So how does one know if two sets of numbers are the same? The answer is simple: check if they have equal values at every index from 0 thru n-1. If anything else happens besides this case (for example: swapping places), they must not be equal after all!

Hash Tables for Characters

Hash tables are an efficient data structure used to store and retrieve data based on keys, which can be any type of value.

Hashing Is the Process of Creating a Table to Map Keys to Values

Hashing is the process of creating a table to map keys to values, such that it's very easy to find an element given its key. In computer science, hashing is used for many different purposes:

- Hashing is used in cryptography to turn data into a fixed-length digest. This makes it easier to verify if two messages are identical without having to re-read all of them.

- Hash tables are frequently used in databases because they allow you to quickly and efficiently search through large amounts of information without reading all the documents at once (or even sequentially).

The Hash Function Takes the Key and Returns an Integer

The hash function takes the key and returns an integer. It should be deterministic, meaning that given the same input, it will always return the same output. It should also be fast; this is one of the main reasons why hash tables aren't used in most programming languages: they're inefficient compared to other data structures like arrays or linked lists.

The Hash Function Generally Uses a Deterministic Algorithm

The hash function generally uses a deterministic algorithm. This means that the same input always produces the same output. Hash functions can create a hash map, allowing you to look up elements in an array by key. Or a hash set allows you to test whether an element is in an array without individually iterating through the whole collection (which is expensive on large collections).

Hash tables are one of the most popular data structures because they offer efficient storage and retrieval of data and constant time performance. Meaning that no matter how often you search for something, it takes roughly the same amount of time every time: O(1).

A Hash Table Uses an Array of Buckets or Slots

A hash table is a data structure that stores data in a way that allows for fast lookup. The key to this structure is using an array of buckets or slots. Each bucket contains some number of slots, and each slot can store one value at a time. The value stored in each slot depends on its position within the array; when you add something new to your hash table, you have to find an empty slot for it using your algorithm (more on this later).

Once you've found an empty slot, you can insert your new item into the hash table by taking its key and performing a mathematical operation called "hashing." It returns another value called an index --and then stores your item with that new index in one of those slots.

Table Size Is Typically a Prime Number to Make a Given Hash Function Have a Better Distribution of Values

A hash table is a data structure that uses an algorithm to store and retrieve data in a particular order. A hash function takes an input of any size, transforms it into a uniform value (typically a number), and then uses this value as an index into an array or other data structure. For example, if we have a set of people's names and want to find their ages, we can create some sort of mapping between names and ages by linking those together with each person's name as the key. Then when someone asks for someone else's age, we just look up their name in the list and return their age. In this way, it's like having your database stored on your computer where every time you want something from it—say "the best vegan sushi restaurant near me"—you simply type what you need into Google instead of having to search through all those menus yourself!

This works because computers quickly search through large databases: if there were 10 million restaurants listed, there would be no problem finding them all! But even though computers are good at looking things up quickly without error (i.e., finding one restaurant randomly), they can still make mistakes sometimes. for example: If we ask our friend Chuck whether he wants Thai food tonight but accidentally write down "Thai" instead of "Didn't." When Chuck sees what we wrote down, he might think incorrectly that I meant Thai food when I meant "didn't." These kinds of errors often happen because people aren't perfect machines yet, but luckily computers aren't either, so they tend not to work well enough together yet!

You Can Use Chaining to Deal with Collisions

If two keys have the same hash, you can use chaining to store them in the same bucket. This is chaining because each element points to its predecessor in the chain. When you delete an element from a hash table with chaining, only those elements whose predecessors are still in the table need to be moved to another bucket. It's a simple concept that works well in practice and is commonly used in hash tables.

Chaining doesn't always work perfectly, though—it has some limitations that should be considered before using it (as we'll see later).

Use Chaining as a Fallback When Two Different Keys Result in the Same Hash Index

One advantage of hashing is that it is possible to use chaining as a fallback when two different keys result in the same hash index. When this happens, both keys are stored in the list and linked together. This technique is called open addressing and uses a linked list to store values. It's also called linear probing because it probes through all possible positions in an array until it finds an available spot for each element or places them on top of one another if there are no spots left.

Open addressing has advantages over other collision resolution methods. It doesn't require rehashing (reassigning everything) or using any extra memory space besides that required for pointers to keep track of where items are stored (as opposed to using something like double-linked lists).

Chapter 8

Skills for Interviews

Learning and Communication Skills

Learning and communication skills are essential for your career if you're a coder. That's especially true when it comes to getting hired for jobs.

Pick the Right Problem

It is important to choose the right problem. First, you should pick a problem that is within your skill level. This way, you can be sure that there are no issues with understanding the problem and its solution. Second, you should pick a problem that interests you so it will be more fun! Thirdly, it needs to be easy to communicate—this means choosing something short enough, so there aren't any complex explanations necessary. Finally, make sure that it can be solved in about 10 minutes or less (the interview clock keeps ticking!).

Use the Right Language

There are a few things to keep in mind regarding language and communicating with your interviewer.

- **Use appropriate language**: You must use the right language for the task. Don't use domain-specific jargon unless necessary (e.g., if there is an established convention for how things are done).

- **Use simple language**: You want your ideas to be concisely expressed, so stick with simple words and sentences as much as possible.

- **Avoid using technical jargon unless necessary**: If you need to dive into technical details, try not to overcomplicate them by using lots of jargon or unfamiliar terms; instead, try simplifying them by breaking down larger concepts into smaller pieces until they become easy enough for everyone present understands

Ask the Right Questions

As a software engineer, you don't know everything. You can't be expected to know the details of every project you've worked on in your career or how the software works. So when your interviewer asks you a question, they're asking, "can you think critically?" Asking questions during an interview gives your interviewer insight into what kind of developer they may have on their hands.

The right kinds of questions that will help show off your critical thinking abilities include:

- Clarifying any confusion about what's being asked

- Understanding the requirements and specifications better so that you can do a better job at solving it

- Understanding what problem is being solved and why it needs to be solved this way (the impact)

Learn to Sketch Your Algorithm

The first thing you'll do in an interview is to sketch your algorithm. You might be nervous, so you should practice as much as possible. If a whiteboard is available, use it! Remember that a whiteboard isn't just for algorithms—you can use it to create diagrams of anything, including graphs and networks if they're relevant to what you're talking about.

If a whiteboard isn't available or you'd prefer not to use one (for example, if there's no room), try practicing on paper instead.

Learn to Talk Through Your Algorithm

Talking through your algorithm is a great way to practice getting used to talking through code. Of course, there are many other ways to do this, including writing out your thoughts on paper or even walking through the algorithm steps in real life.

Think about what you are doing, why you are doing it, and how you are doing it as you talk through your code. Gather feedback from friends who can help point out gaps in your understanding or areas that need more explanation.

Follow a Simple Process to Solve the Problem

The best way to learn how to solve problems is by breaking them down into smaller parts. Once you have broken the problem down, it's easier to see how each part is related and how they fit together.

Think of a problem as a jigsaw puzzle; the more pieces you have, the easier it will be for you to complete your work. If there are no pieces left over after solving an equation or writing code, then it means that all your steps are correct!

When solving technical problems in an interview setting, take time to talk through your process using plain language. This allows others who may not know as much about coding as you can understand what's going on and give feedback if necessary.

Knowledge Migration Skills

You may have heard the term "knowledge migration," but what does it mean? In software engineering and system administration, knowledge migration refers to transferring knowledge between individuals in a team or organization. Knowledge migration aims to ensure that everyone has access to all relevant information to work together effectively as a team.

Knowledge migration involves several steps: identifying what needs to be migrated, determining how best to transfer this information, and training employees on how to use it correctly. Since each company has different processes for managing its data and deciding which pieces are most important for each employee, there's no standard way of doing this across industries or organizations. However, most companies agree that it's important for their employees' roles within the organization (or project) to remain consistent with their current level of expertise. So they can continue contributing successfully at work without disrupting workflow too much from day-to-day tasks like answering questions from other coworkers.

Process

There are two main steps in the process of knowledge migration. The first step involves gathering information about a client's needs and requirements, while the second is defining how the solution will be delivered.

The first step involves determining what you'll be asked to build and gathering all relevant information from your interviewers. This includes understanding who your end users are, what they need from their product or service, and what factors contribute to their success or failure.

You should also be prepared to ask questions at this stage—make sure you understand why certain decisions were made by asking detailed questions about the business processes that led up to them!

Examples of Knowledge Migration

The idea behind knowledge migration is pretty straightforward: it's the process of extracting knowledge from one system and applying it to another system. In other words, if you've learned to do something in one environment or programming language, you can use that knowledge in a new environment without relearning everything.

For example, consider a developer who has worked with Java for several years but has never used C++ before. If this person was hired by an organization that uses C++ exclusively, they might need some time before they can contribute effectively on their first day at work. However, once they have become familiar with both languages' syntaxes and semantics (quite similar), they could quickly become productive again.

Knowledge migration isn't just limited to migrating between programming languages; it can also involve migrating between platforms (e.g., iOS vs. Android) or operating systems (e.g., Windows vs. macOS).

Contribution Analysis Method

Let's say you're tasked with building a web application that allows users to create and manage posts. You're given a rough idea of what the project entails but left to your own devices to solve all the problems involved.

To effectively tackle this problem, you can use the contribution analysis method. This method involves breaking down an entire problem into smaller sub-problems and then assigning each sub-problem a value based on how much time it'll take to solve it. Once this has been done, you'll be able to figure out which sub-problems will impact your overall solution most.

To apply this method in practice, divide your overall product into several components and assign each component's complexity and importance (usually via interviews). Then use these estimates to get a rough idea of where most resources should go; for example: if two components are both equally important but one is more complex than another. Give more resources towards solving that component first because it'll likely make up most of your end product.

Knowledge Migration Is a Critical Skill in a Developer's Career

Knowledge migration is a critical skill in a developer's career. It helps you to be more productive and effective, get promoted faster, get better jobs, and make more money.

Mathematical Modeling Skill

If you've ever written a program that does anything, then you've probably used mathematical modeling.

Why Do We Need Mathematical Modeling?

Mathematical modeling is a powerful tool that can be used to gain insight into the behavior of a system, predict future outcomes, and optimize performance. The process involves creating a simplified representation of reality that allows you to investigate different scenarios under different conditions.

When constructing mathematical models, there are two main things you need to consider: what does the model have to do, and how do we achieve this?

The first question is the most important because it will guide your decision-making. First, it's essential to understand what the model should be used for and what kind of output you want from it. If, for example, your goal is to simulate how an entire system works, then a deterministic model may be more appropriate than a stochastic one.

The second question is also essential because it will help you decide what techniques you need to use and which ones would be most effective. For example, if your goal is to model a complex system with many components and interactions, then constructing the model may be more challenging because more factors are involved.

Suppose your goal is to model a simple system with few components and interactions between them. In that case, constructing the model may be easier because fewer factors are involved.

Modeling in Python

Python is a great language to learn and use. It's easy to read, easy to write and maintain, extendable and deployable.

You can use Python in many ways:

- As a scripting language (e.g., for automation or testing)

- As an object-oriented language on its own

- As a library within another application or framework

Make Your Life Easier with Libraries

As you make your way through the programming world, you will find that some things can make your life much easier. One such thing is libraries.

Libraries are a collection of functions and data structures written by someone else and published for others to use. They're like a box full of tools, each tool being a function or data structure that does something particular (like performing complex mathematical operations). After you've used them once, you'll find yourself reaching for them again and again!

Two main reasons libraries should be used are readability and conciseness. When we write our programs, we use lots of different libraries because they allow us to write code in fewer lines; this is called conciseness.

Divergent Thinking Skills

Divergent thinking is a form of creativity that allows you to generate many original ideas. It's essential for learning, problem-solving, and innovation, but it's also something we do every day without even realizing it.

Divergent thinking is the ability to come up with many different solutions to a problem. This skill is important because it helps kids learn how to solve problems in new and innovative ways.

A good way to help your child develop this skill is by helping them think of many different ways to accomplish a task or use a tool.

Why Is It Important?

Why is it important to be able to think outside of the box? In a world where computers are increasingly capable of performing tasks that were once only possible by humans, being able to solve problems effectively will become increasingly important. Divergent thinking allows you to come up with creative solutions to problems and generate new ideas that can lead to groundbreaking solutions. This skill has been used in diverse fields, including software design, product development, marketing campaigns, and even social change movements.

What are some examples of problems that benefit from divergent thinking? Many jobs require individuals who can generate new ideas on demand. For example:

- Software developers must be able to come up with solutions for potential bugs or flaws in their programs when they arise during testing;

- Designers must constantly come up with innovative ways for companies' brands or products to look more appealing than competitors.

- Marketers need creative ways of promoting their clients' businesses using different media platforms.

- Social activists may need extra-ordinary ways of attracting attention to an issue through protests or rallies

How Do You Improve Your Divergent Thinking Skills?

You can improve your divergent thinking skills by solving as many coding challenges as possible.

If you get stuck, you should also ask for help from friends, classmates, or online communities.

Try to solve the problem differently and take breaks between challenges (even if it's just to get some water or go on a short walk).

If you find yourself getting frustrated, don't give up!

Programming Challenges as a Form of Divergent Thinking Practices

If you're unfamiliar with the concept of divergent thinking, it's a form of thought that allows you to think outside the box. In other words, it's the opposite of convergent thinking. Divergent thinkers can come up with creative and unique solutions to problems by exploring different routes to find solutions. This skill is crucial in coding challenges!

Some examples of divergent thinking practice include:

- Improving problem-solving skills

- Learning new programming languages or frameworks

- Brainstorming ideas for projects

You Can Improve This Important Skill Through Coding Challenges

The ability to think creatively is an important skill for any coder, especially if you're planning on getting a job as a developer. You can improve this important skill through coding challenges.

A coding challenge is a problem that one solves using code, often written in Python or JavaScript. For example, here's one of my favorite coding challenges:

Given two numbers, x and y, write an algorithm that returns true if x is even and false otherwise. If you come up with something like this:

```
def is_even(x): return (x % 2 == 0)
```

You'll have solved the problem correctly! And if someone gives you another number like 2 or 3 or 4 as input instead? Your solution will still work! This means that your solution has been generalized to work with many different inputs beyond just these two numbers—it's a truly good solution because it works well under many different circumstances.

Divergent thinking is an important skill that benefits your career and personal life. It's also a skill that you can improve through coding challenges. The ability to think of multiple solutions to a problem, rather than just one right solution, can help anyone in any profession.

Chapter 9

Interview Cases

Coding interviews are becoming increasingly popular, especially for technical roles. While the traditional interview format assesses your ability to communicate and problem-solve under pressure, a coding interview is designed to assess your technical abilities.

One common format for a coding interview is the case study. In this type of interview, you will be given a real-life scenario and asked to solve it using code. This can be done in any programming language of your choice. The interviewer will be looking to see if you can write code that works, how you approach problem-solving, and whether you can defend your decisions.

Types of Coding Interview Case Studies

There are two main types of coding interview case studies: whiteboarding questions and take-home projects. With a whiteboarding question, you will be given a prompt and asked to solve it on the spot using a whiteboard and marker (or a piece of paper, if you prefer). These questions are usually fairly straightforward and can be solved in less than an hour.

Take-home projects are a bit more involved. For these, you will be given a prompt and a time limit (usually 2-3 hours) to complete the project. Depending on the company's preference, you can do this on your own computer or a provided computer. These case studies are usually more challenging than whiteboarding questions, as they require you to write code that works and think about how your code will scale as the project grows.

Common Prompts for Coding Interview Case Studies

The technical screening test is the most common coding interview case study. This is an assessment the company gives early in the interviewing process, typically before an in-person interview, to weed out candidates who are not technically qualified for the role. Technical screening tests usually consist of multiple-choice questions testing your knowledge of specific programming languages, frameworks, and basic algorithms and data structures. These tests are meant to assess your experience with the technologies relevant to the role you're applying for.

Another common type of coding interview case study is the take-home project. As we mentioned, take-home projects are given to candidates further along in the interviewing process to assess their practical skills. For these projects, you will usually be given 1-2 weeks to complete the project at your own pace (although some companies may have shorter or longer timelines). Take-home projects generally involve building out a small application or feature using the technologies relevant to the role you're applying for. Once you've completed the project, you will often be asked to present your results to an interviewer via video call or in person.

Coding interviews are becoming increasingly popular, especially for technical roles. If you're preparing for an upcoming coding interview, it's important to know what to expect so that you can confidently enter the room!

Inside a Coding Interview Process

Let's see what happens inside a coding interview.

The Candidate Is Given the Assignment to Complete

The candidate is given the problem statement. Then the candidate is given a plain English explanation of the problem and a programming language implementation for solving it.

The candidate is given a few minutes to read through the problem and think about how they will solve it. Then, the candidate has about 15 minutes to write up their solution. Afterward, the interviewer comes back into the room and evaluates their work.

This is a great way to get a sense of how well the candidate understands the problem and whether or not they can write good code. You may have noticed that we didn't give you any specific language here (because it doesn't matter). This is because you can evaluate someone based on their ability to solve problems, not just their technical skills.

The Candidate Is Asked to Complete the Coding Assignment within a Defined Time Frame

You and your team are working on a large project that needs to be finished in three months and shipped to the CEO. You have been given a set of requirements, a deadline, and a budget. You are also working as part of a team that includes an intern and two other developers. In addition, you will have one project manager overseeing your progress and answering any questions you may have. Finally, this whole thing is being sponsored by the CEO himself—he's very interested in seeing what kind of products can be made with this new codebase!

The Candidate Understands the Problem Contextually and Can Outline Potential Solutions

Once you've outlined the problem, it's important to explain how you would approach it. You want to ensure that your candidate understands the problem contextually and can outline potential solutions.

The candidate communicates their approach and asks clarifying questions where necessary.

- The candidate asks clarifying questions as needed.

- The candidate explains their approach in detail and can defend it when asked.

- The candidate could explain how they could have designed the solution differently if they had more time.

The Candidate Feels Comfortable Explaining Their Solution with Examples, Diagrams, and Analogies

You've probably heard "you have to sell yourself" before. This is particularly relevant in technical interviews, where you will often be asked to explain your solution to a problem. In other words, you'll be expected to sell your skills and abilities as an engineer.

The ability to explain your solution is a critical skill for software engineers because it shows that you understand problems at a deeper level than just knowing how to solve them with code (although that's important too). In addition, using examples and analogies can help illustrate why certain approaches work or don't work in different situations—and they can also show off your communication skills!

While it's important to be able to explain your solution, it's also important to know when not to. Sometimes, you may be asked a question that requires specific technical details. In this case, giving as much detail as possible without going overboard or revealing any proprietary information about your current or previous employer is best.

The most important thing to remember is that lying during an interview is never a good idea. Even if you think no one will notice, someone will eventually find out—and your reputation may be irreparably damaged by then.

There's also the possibility that you could miss a question entirely. If this happens, don't panic! It happens to everyone at least once (even if it doesn't seem like it). Just take a deep breath and try again. You can always ask for clarification on any part of the question that doesn't make sense—as long as you don't do this immediately after being asked the question in the first place.

The interview is your chance to shine, so make sure you know exactly what the interviewer wants to hear. If you don't, it will be difficult for them to see how well-qualified you are for the job.

If you're still unsure what to say, try looking up the company's website or social media accounts. This will give you a better idea of what they're all about and how they might feel about certain topics.

If you're still feeling nervous about the interview, try having a friend go through some of your potential answers with you beforehand. This will help ensure that they stick to the key points of your resume and show off the skills that are most important for this particular job.

The Candidate Passes the Assignment with Unit Tests

You have passed the assignment with unit tests. Running your unit tests is a good way to ensure that your code works as intended, but it's also important for another reason: it ensures that your code continues to work as intended after future changes. In addition, unit testing will encourage you to implement a clean design and create reusable functions, which makes future changes easier and quicker!

The more you write, the better you'll get at writing. The same goes for programming: the more you program, the better your code will become. And as it turns out, there are a lot of benefits that come with writing and maintaining code over time!

Writing code forces you to think through every possible scenario and edge case that could come up while using your program. This can help prevent bugs from popping up later down the line. Writing unit tests also ensure that your code continues to work as intended after future changes, which makes future changes easier and quicker! The more you write, the better you'll get at writing.

The Candidate Also Provides a Short Note Explaining Their Approach and How They Could Have Designed the Solution Differently If They Had More Time

In addition to the code, candidates are also asked to provide a short note explaining their approach and how they could have designed the solution differently if they had more time.

The candidate should start by explaining what they did and why they did it this way. Then, they should explain why they could have done things differently or used different algorithms with better performance characteristics (e.g., O(lg n) instead of O(n)). Finally, if there was more time, what would you do differently?

The candidate should also explain how the code improved the original problem statement. For example, they could mention that the code is more efficient or uses less memory than the original solution (e.g., by using a better algorithm).

The candidate should also mention how the solution can be extended or modified to solve other problems in a similar way. For example, the solution could be adapted to solve other types of search problems.

The candidate should also discuss how the code could be improved for future projects. For example, if the solution doesn't scale well with larger inputs, then this could be a problem for real-world applications.

A Coding Interview Differs from a Technical One, But Both Need the Same Skills and Mindset

A coding interview is different from a technical one. Both require skills, but they're not the same skills. A coding interview is about your ability to think and solve problems; it's about your ability to work with others and communicate clearly when explaining what you've done. A technical interview is about how quickly you can learn new tools, how well you can explain them, and whether or not those tools make sense for the project at hand (which may be different than what you were asked about to get hired).

If you're interviewing for a coding position, there's no need to talk about your experience with the technologies used on the job. That's what the interview is for. Instead, think about how those tools could be applied to different problems and what would happen if one tool was replaced.

You should also talk about how you would use those tools on a project and what kinds of projects they're best suited for. For example, if someone asks you about CSS preprocessors, don't just list off the ones you know; talk about why one might be better than another for different situations.

When it comes to technical interviews, you don't have to be perfect. You just have to be better than the rest. When it comes to coding interviews, however, there is no room for mistakes—or even partial understanding of the problem at hand. This can make these interviews quite intimidating for some candidates (and understand why others might avoid them entirely). If you're lucky enough, though, there's a way around all those fears!

Chapter 10

Mock Coding Interviews

Mock coding interviews are interviews that do not count toward an actual job application. Instead, you can practice your problem-solving skills and interview strategy in a controlled environment. You can also test new strategies or technologies to see how you feel about them. Mock interviews tend to be shorter than real interviews. So if you're going to use a programming language for the first time, it's wise to choose one like Python or Ruby, which has many libraries available for solving common problems such as sorting data or parsing JSON into objects. Even though mock coding interviews don't count in the real world, they can help improve your chances of success when it comes time for the real thing - especially if you prepare beforehand with what might happen during your interview!

Mock Coding Interviews Are Interviews That Do Not Count Toward an Actual Job Application

Mock coding interviews are a great way to practice your technical skills and get comfortable talking about them in an interview setting. They're not a final job application but rather a chance to run through questions you might encounter on the job. A mock coding interview is typically shorter than a real one, giving you more time to ask your interviewer questions. It also allows your interviewer to give feedback on how well you did so that there are no surprises when it's time for the real thing!

You can do these mock interviews over the phone or in person with someone who will play the role of an interviewer (that could be anyone from an experienced friend or family member all the way up through professional interview coaches).

The best way to prepare for coding interviews is to practice them! So don't wait until you get the call from your dream job—start preparing now.

You don't need to be a coding wizard to land an amazing job in tech. All you need is some basic interview prep, a few practice rounds with potential interviewers, and the confidence that comes from knowing you're as prepared as possible for your next career step.

They Are an Opportunity to Practice Your Problem-Solving Skills and Interview Strategy in a Controlled Environment

One of the most important aspects of coding interviews is solving problems. Unfortunately, problem-solving skills don't come easily and can be difficult to practice without having a problem in front of you. Mocking your code interviews allows you to work through this process in a controlled environment where mistakes are not only allowed but expected!

Mocking code interviews also provide an opportunity for candidates to exercise their interview strategy as well as their coding skills. For example, if a candidate has conducted research about the company or role before their mock interview, it will give them greater confidence when answering questions during the actual interview.

Mocking code interviews are also a great way for candidates to build their confidence in their coding skills. This is especially valuable for those who do not have experience interviewing with companies like Google or Facebook because they can get used to the process and learn how best to prepare themselves.

In addition to these benefits, mock interviews are also a great way for candidates to practice answering specific types of questions they will be asked during their actual interview. For example, suppose a candidate is interviewing with a company that emphasizes data structures and algorithms. In that case, they can consider this knowledge when preparing for their mock interview by reading up on these topics before the session.

You Can Also Test New Strategies or Technologies to See How You Feel about Them

One of the best parts of a mock coding interview is that you can try out new strategies or new technologies to see how you feel about them. For example, you might have heard that functional programming is the future, but what if it isn't? What if you don't like it? It's good practice to test out a new strategy or technology before jumping into something in your day job.

Using techniques and methodologies that are not a regular part of your job is also good practice. This can include using different languages and approaching problems from a different perspective (e.g., top-down instead of bottom-up). And also thinking about problems differently (e.g., recursively vs. iteratively), etc.

One way to practice this is to do a mock technical interview with someone who knows less about programming or technology than you do. This will force you to explain some of the basics of your work, and it can give you a better understanding of what people outside your field think about programming.

Mock Interviews Tend to Be Shorter Than Real Interviews, So If You're Going to Use a Programming Language for the First Time, It's Wise to Choose a Very Simple One Like Python or Ruby

So you've decided to add mock interviews to your practice routine. If so, great! Mock interviews tend to be shorter than real interviews, so if you're going to use a programming language for the first time, it's wise to choose a very simple one like Python or Ruby.

You can focus on the syntax or semantics of the language rather than worrying about memory leaks and other technicalities. The point is not to get hung up on details; rather, try and make sure that you understand everything in each answer without having to refer back multiple times before arriving at an answer (though this depends heavily on how many questions are asked).

The point of a mock interview is not to get hung up on details; rather, try and make sure that you understand everything in each answer without having to refer back multiple times before arriving at an answer.

Suppose you're going to practice using a database. In that case, you should use SQLite because it doesn't need the overhead of setting up an account with an external database service and connecting your application to it. It's a lightweight database that is easy to install and use. If your interviewer asks about the differences between SQLite and MySQL or Postgres, tell him that those databases are much more powerful than SQLite but can also be complicated if they're not used properly.

Even Though Mock Coding Interviews Don't Count in the Real World, They Can Help Improve Your Chances of Success When It Is Time for the Real Thing

It's important to remember that mock interviews are not real interviews. They're more like practice sessions where you can learn new programming languages, technologies, and problem-solving strategies. But they're not just for beginners! Even experienced programmers who've done hundreds of interviews will benefit from mock coding interviews.

You should also remember that the interviewers won't always be as skilled as you are at their jobs. They may ask trick questions or otherwise try to throw you off your game—so don't get frustrated if everything doesn't go smoothly! It's okay to take a few minutes before answering a question so that you can think about it clearly and answer accurately (instead of rushing through an answer).

A Mock Coding Interview Is Like a Dress Rehearsal for a Play - It Gives You Space to Work through Issues before They Matter

The goal of a mock coding interview is to give you some practice before the real thing. It's like a dress rehearsal for a play: you get to try out your lines and see how they sound in front of an audience without consequences. You can also work out any issues with teammates or technology before they become problems during the interview!

In addition to helping you improve your chances of success when it comes time for the real thing, mock interviews help you build confidence through repetition. Which can positively affect other parts of your life—including work performance and relationships with colleagues and partners outside work.

A mock interview is a chance to practice your skills in an interview setting. You can use these questions to get comfortable with the format and, if you're looking for a job, learn what questions are most likely to come up during one.

So you want to be a programmer? It's not easy, but it's worth it.

Conclusion

We hope you've enjoyed our guide to coding interviews and feel confident about your upcoming interview! We know that for many of us, it's stressful enough just to have a job interview—let alone one with a technical component. But we also know that if you put in the work, you can ace these kinds of interviews. And we want to help you do that!

We're not going to lie this is not a comprehensive list of questions you might be asked at your next coding interview. There are literally countless ways that companies can ask questions—and even more possible answers—that will test your knowledge and skills. However, if you take the time to learn how to solve problems using the same techniques that professional developers use daily, you'll be ready for anything they throw at you. And that's what this guide is all about: helping you become a better coder by equipping yourself with the tools necessary to succeed in today's competitive job market.

Go forth and conquer!

References

Alvesson, Mats, and Dan Kärreman. 2007. "Constructing mystery: Empirical matters in theory development." Academy of management review 32 (4):1265-1281.

Anderson, Ross C, Meg Guerreiro, and Joanna Smith. 2016. "Are all biases bad? Collaborative grounded theory in developmental evaluation of education policy."

Journal of Multidisciplinary Evaluation 12 (27):44-57.

Creswell, John W, and Cheryl N Poth. 2017. Qualitative inquiry and research design: Choosing among five approaches: Sage publications.

Miles, Matthew B, A Michael Huberman, and Johnny Saldana. 2013. Qualitative data analysis: A methods sourcebook. Thousand Oaks, CA: SAGE Publications, Incorporated. 26

Miles, Matthew B., and Michael A. Huberman. 1994. Qualitative Data Analysis. 2nd edition ed. Thousand Oaks, CA.: Sage

Sinkovics, Rudolf R., Elfriede Penz, and Pervez N. Ghauri. 2008. "Enhancing the Trustworthiness of Qualitative Research in International Business." Management International Review 48 (6):689-714. doi: 10.1007/s11575-008-0103-z.